The  to
GLOBAL
SURVEILLANCE

'Publishers have created lists of short books that discuss the questions that your average [electoral] candidate will only ever touch if armed with a slogan and a soundbite. Together [such books] hint at a resurgence of the grand educational tradition... Closest to the hot headline issues are *The No-Nonsense Guides*. These target those topics that a large army of voters care about, but that politicos evade. Arguments, figures and documents combine to prove that good journalism is far too important to be left to (most) journalists.'

Boyd Tonkin,
The Independent,
London

About the author
Born in London, Robin Tudge has lived and worked in Moscow, Hanoi and Beijing, and as a journalist has written for scores of publications worldwide. His first book was the pioneering *Bradt Guide to North Korea* in 2003, then in 2005 he co-wrote the best-selling *Rough Guide to Conspiracy Theories*. A lifelong fascination with police states and surveillance became focused on the contemporary situation in 2006, when the British government legislated for UK citizens to start carrying ID cards. He is also an aspiring actor, living in Deptford, within sight of where the playwright and spy Kit Marlowe was cut down.

Acknowledgements
The author would like to thank the following for their generosity, patience and support in making this book possible with their constructive comment, direction, insights and patience, starting with Troth Wells and Chris Brazier at New Internationalist, Helen Wallace at Genewatch, Guy Herbert and Phil Booth at NO2ID and all the other campaigners there who suggested good reads, particularly Linda Welsh. Along the way were many who had the patience to give feedback on the text, provide info or just listen to me going on about it, so I give great thanks to Andrew Lockett, Ben Cummins, Sakura Tanaka, Matt Smith, Henry Porter, Simon Thorne and everyone at Platts, Nick Bonner, Colin and Ruth Tudge, Gus Hosein, Judith Vidal Hall, Peter Hogg, Zac Stringer, Richard and Sangita Hunt, Steve Wangford, James McConnachie, Jerry Goodman, Dr Tom Hawkins and Dr Gardner Thompson, the Barretts, the Coopers and the Burns. I'd especially like to thank my wife Dawn Tudge for her unending support and enthusiasm for the book from its inception to its publication.

About the New Internationalist
New Internationalist is an independent, not-for-profit publishing co-operative that reports on issues of global justice. We publish informative current affairs and popular reference titles, complemented by multicultural recipe books, photography and fiction from the Global South, as well as calendars, diaries and cards – all with a global justice world view.

If you like this *No-Nonsense Guide* you will also enjoy the *New Internationalist* magazine. The freshly designed magazine is packed full of quality writing, in-depth analysis and new features, including:
- Agenda: cutting-edge reports
- Argument: heated debate between experts
- Analysis: understanding the key global issues
- Action: making change happen
- Alternative living: inspiring ideas
- Arts: the best of global culture.

To find out more about the **New Internationalist**, visit our website at **www.newint.org**

The **NO-NONSENSE GUIDE** to

GLOBAL
SURVEILLANCE

Robin Tudge

NewInternationalist

The No-Nonsense Guide to Global Surveillance
Published in the UK in 2010 by New Internationalist™ Publications Ltd
55 Rectory Road
Oxford OX4 1BW, UK
www.newint.org
New Internationalist is a registered trade mark.

Cover image: Getty Images

Series editor: Chris Brazier
Design by New Internationalist Publications Ltd.

Printed in UK by Bell and Bain Ltd.
who hold environmental accreditation ISO 14001.

Mixed Sources
Product group from well-managed
forests and other controlled sources
www.fsc.org Cert no. TT-COC-002769
© 1996 Forest Stewardship Council
FSC

British Library Cataloguing-in-Publication Data.
A catalogue record for this book is available from the British Library.

Library of Congress Cataloguing-in-Publication Data.
A catalogue for this book is available from the Library of Congress.

ISBN 978-1-906523-84-8

Foreword

PRIVACY IS THE human right upon which many other rights rest. Privacy and free expression, the ability to live, think and voice one's thoughts freely: these are all inter-dependent concepts linked to the dignity of the individual. Yet the threat to privacy in the modern era has never been greater. Governments, corporations and cybercriminals are among others orchestrating the trans-border flow and harvesting of our personal data. They may be interested in combating terrorism and organized crime, in promoting interactivity and profiling for advertising, in perpetrating fraud or worse. But all work, both knowing and unknowingly, towards the ultimate marginalization of the most fragile right of privacy.

We at Privacy International believe that privacy forms part of the bedrock of freedoms. Since our organization was founded in 1990, our goal has always been to create protections and laws at national and international levels to preserve it. We have hundreds of leading experts in privacy and human rights from around the world, including computer professionals, academics, lawyers, journalists and human rights activists working globally to defend personal privacy against the ever-growing and morphing forms of privacy violations. Our team consists of libertarians and liberals, conservatives and progressives. We have worked in environments as diverse as refugee camps in eastern Africa to engineering hubs in Silicon Valley. We liaise with policy-makers and civil society in dozens of countries, as we work to promote strong safeguards that apply equally to international organizations and complex economies, to developing countries and emerging legal systems.

One of the more worrying developments we are seeing is just how difficult it is to monitor those who push surveillance technologies. In 1995 PI reviewed some 240 Western companies, some of them household

names, that since the 1970s had been selling surveillance technology to some of the most oppressive,
murderous police and military states. This technology
enabled the genocide in Rwanda, and allowed the
South African apartheid regime to function as it did.
The companies that supplied Guatemala's dictators
knew what their products were going to be used for
– the deathlist targets were on the tender documents.
Many of these 240 companies have since begun to
'consult' with telecommunications companies, internet service providers, governments, lawmakers and
regimes to build surveillance from the core, 'by
design'. Meanwhile, many non-Western firms, notably
from China, are beginning to move into the global
surveillance industry and sell their wares for the
enhancement of surveillance states worldwide.

The defense of privacy is not easy, but the fact
that privacy has turned into an issue that is on the
front pages of news and media sources worldwide is
testament to the importance of the task. The reams
of communiqués we receive daily, from public and
parliaments alike, show how alive the issue of privacy
is and how vital is its defense.

This well-written, forceful overview provides an
excellent introduction to the history and contemporary issues of the world of surveillance and shows
how we are all affected by its exponential growth –
whether we want to be or not.

Gus Hosein
Senior Fellow, Privacy International

CONTENTS

Introduction

A 2007 REPORT by international NGO Privacy International rated the world's states in terms of surveillance. It assessed how extensive or endemic was the surveillance and what workable safeguards in law defended the privacy of these spied-upon citizens. One might not be surprised to find China and Russia listed among the states with the most 'endemic' surveillance. But at this top table was also placed China's democratic brother and nemesis, Taiwan, those roaring capitalist outposts Malaysia and Thailand, and those bastions of democracy and freedom, the US, the UK and France.*

Surveillance is essentially an over-arching means of accruing and sifting information. It is indispensable for an organization or entity of any complexity, from the village to the nation-state, from the corner shop to the transnational corporation, from the local church to the Vatican, to keep account – nothing can function without knowledge. As societies have grown more complex and individuals' interactions with the state and one another have become entrenched and deepened, the technology of surveillance has expanded to global proportions, from satellite-enabled Global Positioning Systems right down to the near-atomic level of one's DNA.

Endemic surveillance underpinned communist states and military dictatorships paranoid about stifling dissent – but, as a tool of accounting, surveillance runs throughout the capitalist and social-democratic states of the West as well. And while espionage, citizen monitoring and censorship have undoubtedly enabled the jackbooted to stamp their authority and extend their power, they have also been vital tools for opposing authoritarianism in war and defending 'freedom' in peace. This book is interested in surveillance in its civilian contexts, where it will often be seen that the military and intelligence services were the originators of some technique that was then developed for wide-spread use against civilians. Too often, and even with the best intentions, a surveillance system temporarily developed to defend freedom has become a permanent, embedded threat to human rights and democracy.

Surveillance is often a means of retaining and enhancing profit and power, whether on the part of an expansive empire or a desperate regime. Where once it was a means to an end it has now become an end in itself. The logarithms and artificial intelligence systems of computerized databases have gone from sifting the data so as to enable an outcome, to being trusted to direct that outcome. Surveillance is too often adapted from being an accounting tool to one that governments and corporations will use to direct and pre-empt.

The vast array of databases of information about individuals, be they state or private, social welfare or social networking, are usually set up to be siloed or self-contained, but are being rapidly shared and converged, mostly in unseen, unreported and unaccountable ways. This sharing is justified or sold to the citizen-consumer as being for their own good, their better security, their health, or even their fun. From Facebook via the 'War on Terror' to the war on plastic bags, the shrill voices of governments and marketing companies exhort us to hand over more data and allow it to be shared – though often we are not told what is happening until it's too late. Information systems of unprecedented power and potential danger are being created, yet in a time of unprecedented global prosperity.

The road to Hell is paved with good intentions. Every new dollop of data allows government workers – confident in their own ability to run the system better – to adapt existing systems, to salvage something from the ruins of a costly, failed experiment, or to clear up the problems created by a previous 'brilliant' solution. Or just to accrue more power in the phenomenon known as 'function creep'. In the private sector, money can't be made without the use of and then sale of data, which is 'just business, nothing personal'. Meanwhile, the key to profit, power and stable sexual relationships is seen to be loyalty and good behavior. How loyal are your customers and citizens? How faithful will they be in good times and bad? How far are they guided by their genes or their upbringing – and can enough data be accrued to predict and pre-empt their behavior?

Most brilliant new solutions involve a database of some kind, but data about the average Briton, for example, is on about 700 databases – and who could name even 10 of those databases? Concepts like consent and privacy are ground into dust by a thousand spinning hard-drives owned by public and private agencies whose interests and operating philosophy have converged.

Citizens, meanwhile, have become atomized within a globalized society. They are becoming less reliant on themselves or their communities than on a technology-based ether that demands every electron of their data just so that they can function. Every problem this creates demands another (profitable) techno-solution, and one which often involves yet more surveillance...

Step by step, a vast, utterly undemocratic enterprise is created, in which people are told they have 'nothing to hide, nothing to fear', but through which they are expected to stand naked before their watchers, in real time, for all time. Concepts like the presumption of innocence are binned – people are suspected until they can prove otherwise.

So surveillance goes from being a tool of accounting to one of calling to account, and God is replaced by Google.

Robin Tudge
London

1 A day in the life...
'Big Brother' today

We are only now waking up to the implications of living in a world where surveillance of us is entirely routine. The chapter begins with a fictional glimpse of an ordinary life in a modern Western city in the near future. It then looks at how spying has become a normal aspect of society rather than a dangerous game played by professional spooks – and at how internet phenomena such as Facebook and Google have led us voluntarily to hand over our most personal details.

ONE SUNNY LATE afternoon, Frank leaves his city home, preparing to take his daughter and her friends to soccer practice. His next-door neighbors' child is staring at him through their front-room window, as he often does. A strange lad who never says hello, whose staring Frank finds a little unnerving, but not enough – yet – to demand an Anti-Social Behavior Order of the kind he has read about in the news-plasma. Frank used to stare back, but then he noticed the CCTV camera atop the new porch next door and realized it would contain video of him staring at the boy – which could lead to Frank being considered the antisocial one and to his home being raided.

Frank takes the recycling bag with him to the bin, conscious that today is the recycling day – he got it wrong a month ago and the council emailed him, promising a fine and penalty points on his ID card if he offended again. Frank doesn't know that it was the boy next door, on the council payroll as a 'Junior Streetwatcher', who tipped off the council and sent them porch-CCTV footage of Frank's misdemeanor. However, the grateful council thereby noted the new porch and, having checked GoogleEarth for further works and extensions on the house, would soon upgrade the boy's house to a higher tax band.

Frank doesn't mind driving his daughter Abigail and friends to soccer, but resents having had to pay for the privilege by registering with the Vetting and Barring List to prove he was not unsuitable to be near children. Abigail needs to do extra sports to stabilize her Body Mass Index since the school nurse declared her three kilos on the 'wrong side of obese' (as the school's warning email put it). Also, her confidence was knocked when her SkoolCanteen card refused to allow her to buy french fries – something the canteen till worker felt compelled to point out loud enough for all the other schoolchildren to hear.

Abigail asks why Alan, the father of her friend Janine, doesn't drive them as he used to. Frank explains that Alan had tweeted support for an anti-airport protest group and got himself disbarred from driving within three miles of an airport for six months. Alan had found out about this only when police pulled him over, having tracked his car through the Advanced Number Plate Recognition system. Alan was later thrown off the Metro for coming within range of the City airport (the Radio Frequency Identifier on his ID card being picked up by Metro 'listening' posts). Alan knows (but can't prove) these restrictions have cost him freelance work. What he does not know is that his ban is effectively indefinite, since the Borders Agency will not let him leave the country – governments worldwide are listing all protestors alongside window-smashing anarchists and sex tourists as personae non gratae. Alan's suitability for volunteer work with children is also damaged by default and he is only a few mouse clicks away from the disparaging lies put on his Experian file by an ex-colleague. Frank hopes that friendship with Alan does not render him 'guilty' by association – suspicion suffices these days to shut down people's lives.

As he drives the car past the local delis, cafés and restaurants, Frank notes the absence of the feral youths who once plagued this strip. Since it was SafeZoned™ the youths now mostly keep to their housing estate, having succumbed to the shouting CCTV and Tescapo hassling them every time they 'ganged' anywhere, as well as to the loss of extra-curricular school activities and revoking of their parents' welfare benefits. Anyway, their PayCards work only in predetermined areas – if they have no means to do business somewhere, they literally have no business being there, and can be moved on. An evening out without ID cards is a criminal one. But Frank notes that, when SafeZoned™ was introduced, local property prices spiked almost $25,000 overnight.

Frank ponders that the paranoiacs and dissenters against this kind of surveillance (people rarely heard from these days, curiously) always overlooked the benefits when the schemes were first proposed. Surely if you had nothing to hide, you had nothing to fear. But Frank, like everyone, knows someone whose Amex CityPass/Oyster PayWave/ID has been DEN-ID at the supermarket or post office. This has required them to contact The Administrator and launched them into days or even weeks of hassle trying to sort out the problem – very, very difficult when dealing with bureaucrats who do not believe who you are without a valid ID card.

Indeed, just that morning, Frank's work computer was stuffed by repeated biometric recognition failures. The IT worker contacted BioTrack, which revealed that Frank's biometrics were in use in Thailand – his credit card had been cloned a few weeks before – and that a man with a suspicious medical record and even more suspicious partner was being held in Bangkok police custody in connection with the cloning (how BioTrack knew that, it did not say). However, Frank's insurance would not cover any bioclone crimes in the meantime.

'Big Brother' today

Frank knows that forever after a database will exist somewhere linking the events to his name and could make his next holiday abroad very, very risky.

These thoughts sprinkled into Frank's mind as he sat at his desk and manifested as a grimace, which was duly noted by his computer's Webcam and fed back to the company Stress Detector. Already, the company Voice Stress Detector had picked up enough negative inflections over the past month to trigger a warning fired from the SWEAT (Stress Warning Early Alert Team) program to his manager. This VSD note of stress, if matched with his father's high blood pressure and his uncle's heart disease, could suggest worse health to come, raising Frank's health premiums, stalling his advancement at work, and further stressing him out.

All this makes Frank want a cigarette, but he has given up. He wonders if maybe he too should take up a sport, thereby earning more health insurance premium reductions. Frank has already told his insurance provider that he doesn't smoke, so buying any cigarettes now would hoick his premiums and mark him as a lying recidivist. Meanwhile, a sneaky cigarette won't do, as Face Recognition and Behavior Camera footage on CCTV would link his smoking to his file. He pulls into the sports ground and parks. As the girls gambol out of the car, he thinks, 'It wasn't like this when I was young'...

How did hyper-surveillance come to seem so normal?

All of the facets of the hyper-surveillance outlined above are either in situ or are being planned, having been set up on the sly, with systems and laws sold to the public with some espoused benefit masking ulterior agendas or motives. How has this hyper-surveillance come to be normalized, and with such surprising ease, as consumers have allowed themselves to be invited and lured in?

Spying is becoming a normal profession and a part of all our lives. The US National Security Agency was not revealed until the 1970s, while Britain's secret services MI5 and MI6 were unmentionables until the 1990s, with recruitment involving Oxbridge undergraduates being 'sniffed at by wolves'. Now these agencies, along with the FBI and the CIA, freely advertise jobs in newspapers and online. Intelligence agencies have taken a strategic decision to raise their profiles over the years, so as to garner more public support, funding and laws in their favor. Spies themselves are open to career change. Former CIA director George HW Bush made it into the White House, ex-KGB bureau chief Vladimir Putin made it to be president and prime minister of Russia, while former MI5 boss Stella Rimington is a novelist and expert pundit. One might conclude that spies have come to run the place.

But the technology of surveillance is now globally accessible, with the internet instantly disseminating data to the world, often without the consent or control of its subjects. This is an extraordinary, very recent development that is nonetheless becoming normalized for many people, especially the young. Online shopping and social networking are two areas that have made the web integral to many if not most people's daily functioning. Meanwhile, personal-disclosure websites such as Facebook invite us both to snoop on others and to disclose way more than might otherwise be considered wise – hyper-exhibitionism has been first glamorized and then normalized.

Big Brother – from Orwell to reality TV

Many commentators complain that the world is stumbling into something comparable to *Nineteen Eighty-Four*, evoking George Orwell's tale of authoritarian hyper-surveillance and oppression under the God-like leader of The Party and dictator of Oceania,

'Big Brother' today

Big Brother. Orwell's Big Brother is revered and feared, spending all His time Watching You. But today Big Brother is synonymous with the global TV show that imprisons a handful of nobodies who fart and flirt for several weeks under 24/7 surveillance and are rewarded with fame and riches. One contestant on the format sold to over 70 countries worldwide was told on air that she had cancer. Her remaining days on Earth duly became public property.

Big Brother (BB) has shifted from a social experiment into how strangers in a confined space might interact into a series of convoluted tortures and mind games dreamed up by faceless producers. It exemplifies the intoxication of power and blind pursuit of ratings-profit. Its impact, as behavioral expert and BB commentator Jenni Trent Hughes noted, has been to make schoolchildren's ambitions now just 'to be famous'[1] – or indeed infamous, as BB has spearheaded the presentation of outrageous behavior as something to be celebrated. This is ironic, because the reality for most people of enveloping surveillance that focuses on the atomic minutiae of life is to catch them doing wrong.

For all that a few have profited by BB, many more will fall by following its example. They do it on the web, making fools of themselves in fleeting fits and flights of fancy with comments or photos that they forget in an instant, but will be remembered forever in a cached file somewhere in the world. Somehow web-users perceive their readers to be as distant and virtual as the web itself and so freely cross normal boundaries of behavior, forgetting that the absence of face-to-face opprobrium does not mean there will be no offline comeback some day.[2] Even President Obama felt moved to warn a group of teenagers to be careful about their Facebook postings, 'because in the YouTube age, whatever you do, it will be pulled up again later somewhere in your life... When you're young, you make mistakes and you do some stupid stuff.'[3] Or, as a frustrated father told his son who was broadcasting his own tantrum online: 'You're making an ass of yourself for all eternity!'[4]

Even the masters of the secret services have fallen victim to the easy allure of uploading something to the internet on a whim. Personal information about the new head of Britain's MI6, Sir John Sawers, including his numerous home addresses, his children, movements and contacts with senior diplomats, were left open to the world on his wife's Facebook page as she had not added privacy settings.[5] Oxford University staff use Facebook to find photographic proof of students breaking university rules.[6] The judge in the trial of a 20-year-old driver who crashed and severely injured a woman, saw Facebook photos of the defendant at a Halloween party dressed as a prisoner, calling himself Jail Bird. Where another defendant accused of this offense might have got a fine, he received two years in jail for his 'depraved' behavior.[7] Canadian Nathalie Blanchard was on long-term sick leave with depression from her job at IBM in Quebec. But insurance giant Manulife found Facebook 'photos of her having fun', concluded that she was therefore fit to work and her benefits were stopped.[8]

Meanwhile, the Facebook application 'What's Your Actual Age?' promises to 'determine the real age of your body based on lifestyle, environmental, and social factors'. Users give information they would baulk at telling their doctor, then this is funneled away (who knows where) for profitable sifting through by any insurer or agency with access. Facebook may have some privacy proscriptions on data sharing, but these do not apply to applications. Meanwhile, Facebook is hackable like anything else, as when, in 2005, two MIT students downloaded the data from 70,000 profiles as part of a project. Still, over 500 million users worldwide – almost a tenth of the global population – are handing personal data to Facebook, creating a model of social-networking that dwarves anything the Stasi or CIA might have dreamed of. Facebook also may use information collected 'from other sources, including but not limited to newspapers and internet sources such as blogs, instant messaging services and other users of Facebook, to supplement your profile' – probably from Google.

Google's sinister reach

Social portals like Facebook at least partly allow user control over what they exhibit – Google however, a company of staggering reach in its fact-finding, its global renown and market power, reveals to the world everything else there is to know, whether they like it or not. To 'google' someone is now common practice and parlance, although some consider it stalking (as much can be said of sites like www.192.com – if you're worried you can use www.ziggs.com to see who's been googling you).

A permanent record of every word put into Google Search is retained, whether your motive be murder or just fleeting curiosity. In 2005, computer consultant Robert Petrick was found guilty of first-degree murder of his wife Sutphe, following evidence that he had typed words like 'neck', 'snap', break' and 'hold' into Google's search bar, and called up articles on body decomposition and the topography of the lake where her body was found.[9]

Google Mail users sign a 'privacy agreement' licensing Google to use email contents to provide 'relevant advertising'. Google Latitude allows users to turn their cellphones into personal GPS trackers enabling friends and family to track them. Google Earth and Google Street Finder enable the world to look into your back garden and through your front window, although government buildings in Washington DC and London have been removed for providing too much reconnaissance data for terrorists. Google is also developing an App for companies to crunch through employee reviews, promotions and pay histories to predict who might be most likely to quit.[10]

The prospect of someone's employer pre-emptively discovering their disloyalty would surely make people's need for privacy all the more acute – but the meme 'nothing to hide, nothing to fear' might then be applied to them, leaving them suspected of anything from a drug habit to an affair. People whose partners won't sign up to Google Mobile and allow them-selves to be tracked everywhere – a service that the police and secret services access freely – could also be assumed to have 'something to hide'. Private detective agencies could then fill the gap, surreptitiously install-ing software onto targets' mobile phones to track them and every call and text they make. Love Detector services will phone up your lover, interrogate them about their feelings for you and analyze their voice for lies. Meanwhile, www.getcheckmate.com supplies kits for checking their underwear for semen stains.

Journalism as spycraft

Maybe it's no surprise that many private eyes are former surveillance, military and police officers, catering to the suspicious, inspired and succored by the sensationalizing of the salacious by the press. Gutter journalism has long been well served by tech-nology in its thirst for tittle-tattle, gossip and scandal. This has been so ever since the 'detective cameras' of the 1880s took fast, discreet photos of people in public, rendering obsolete the studio images that indi-viduals could control.[11]

Journalism mirrors spycraft. Reporters disguise themselves to stalk subjects or go undercover into political groups and workplaces, sitting in cars for days, staking out subjects' homes with telephoto lenses. Journalists rummage through targets' trash cans and trawl though their phone bills, or employ private investigators to hack into their cellphone voicemails. They befriend, bribe, sweet-talk and bully targets' friends, colleagues, family and acquaintances for information or filch what they can from Google, Facebook, Twitter or whatever iApp Foursquare throws up.

Trawling the trash cans can turn up real gems, as when Britain's *Sunday Times* found the memos Tony Blair wrote about weapons of mass destruction before the Iraq War. But another British News Corporation rag, *The News of the World*, was rumbled for having bugged the phone of some 3,000 noteworthies, including politicians, footballers and PR gurus, and possibly one former Metropolitan police chief, with private investigators hacking into cellphone messages, duping telephone companies into handing over confidential information and seeking bank statements and tax records.

Unfortunately the onset of ID cards and fathomless personal reference checking will likely make undercover journalism very difficult, if not impossible. One Bloomberg journalist was had up before his managers following harassing calls from libel lawyers Carter-Ruck, acting for oil trading company Trafigura – which had been dumping toxic waste in Africa – after he, like tens of thousands of others, had simply tweeted his view on the story to his friends. London's Metropolitan Police also trawls Twitter, Facebook, Flickr and blogs, with Radian 6 and Metrix 6 software from 6consulting used to help the force control its 'corporate brand'.[12] Similarly, Wikipedia's Scanner device can match the 40 million edits to the net address of the editor – showing up that some of Wikipedia's entries are written by the CIA.[13]

Some news stories are really leaks and smears given out by the surveillance business. Former US ambassador Joseph Wilson sought to refute the claims of the

George W Bush administration that Iraq had a nuclear enrichment program. The White House tried to silence Wilson by exposing his wife Valerie Plame as a CIA agent, ending her career and endangering her life. Using the press for careericide by smear was standard practice for the original FBI boss, J Edgar Hoover, who himself had a startlingly burlesque private life but who obsessively orchestrated the destruction via smear campaigns of anyone of whom he disapproved.

That so demented a man as Hoover, whose abuse of power in public office was at odds not only with his own values but with those of the American democracy he was supposedly defending, could attain such a position of power was extraordinary, but such is the potential for abuse by the practitioners of surveillance. The toxic combination of suppressed eroticism and unbridled, murderous megalomania – backed by a supposedly sunny ideology – puts him on a par with his Nazi contemporary, Heinrich Himmler, chief of history's most frightening police apparatus.

A run through the history of surveillance will show how often epic systems of spying and control have been used to destroy individuals on whatever pretext is available, true or invented.

1 http://nin.tl/alZVdP 2 http://nin.tl/cJbxhU 3 http://nin.tl/9hjF7D 4 Play him off, Keyboard Cat! YouTube. 5 BBC news online, 5 July 2009. 6 http://nin.tl/arklb7 7 http://nin.tl/bSNFln 8 http://nin.tl/dcn7J8 9 http://nin.tl/9qYSzq 10 http://nin.tl/cKCLIX 11 http://nin.tl/bLfcQk 12 http://nin.tl/9AkIL7 13 http://news.bbc.co.uk/1/hi/6947532.stm

2 A brief history of surveillance

Rulers throughout the ages have devised systems for monitoring their citizens – often to ensure they can be taxed. But through the centuries the thirst for surveillance of people's conduct and opinions has intensified as the technology has improved. The Spanish Inquisition, the French Revolutionary Terror, the totalitarian states of Hitler and Stalin: all of these could only dream of the possibilities for surveillance accorded by today's electronic world.

THE FIRST BOOK of the Christian Bible (and the Jewish Torah) shows how long-seated in the human psyche, and foremost in the mind of the storyteller, is the notion of surveillance. In the Garden of Eden, Adam and Eve's first crime was to disobey the Word of God and eat the forbidden fruit. The problem was that it made Adam and Eve aware of their nakedness and, worried that they might be being watched, they wore figleaves over their genitals. God, being omniscient, saw the whole thing but forced confessions from the pair and had Adam denounce Eve, who was duly cursed, and the serpent of temptation that had bade them eat the fruit. For this, they were deported from Eden. Elsewhere, the angel Lucifer was conspiring against God, also meriting his deportation from Heaven and his rebranding as the Prince of Darkness. Darkness is a bad thing because it veils undisclosed activities, and anything that needs doing in darkness is, one is invited to suspect, evil. God, and later on Jesus Christ, brings light to the world – and light is good because it allows everything and everyone to be watched.

So at least since the Bible was written, the perception of being watched over and the self-directing need to be seen to comply with the law has been evident in the human psyche. The Book of Job puts it so: 'For His eyes are on the ways of man, And He sees all his steps, There is no darkness nor shadow of death Where the workers of iniquity may hide themselves.'[1] The Qur'an puts it similarly: 'Most surely your Lord is watching'.[2]

The idea that an account is being kept somewhere of your every deed is widely entrenched. Traditionally, Christians expect upon death to be greeted at the Gates of Heaven by St Peter, who will judge their worthiness to enter heaven based on a fat file of their life's deeds, good and bad. This concept of a file for the Day of Reckoning keeps them on the straight and narrow. An earthly parallel was created in 1086 by William the Conqueror, who sent agents across his new fiefdom of England to determine exactly who owned what land, people and livestock, and to ensure the state recouped the taxes owed to him (*plus ça change*). These accounts, for which there was no appeal nor correction, were duly compiled into a single tome, on the basis of which costly or life-threatening penalties were meted out upon William's subjects. This 'strict and terrible last account', as one writer called it over a century later,[3] was commonly known as The Domesday Book – the book of the Day of Doom, the Day of Judgment, for it allowed a centralized bureaucracy to visit damnation upon Earth... and that was just about tax.

Surveillance through to the Middle Ages

The hallmark of every civilization from Ancient Egypt and Babylon onwards was the ability to record the assets and transactions of the state, to have a functioning bureaucracy acting as a 'kind of grand scheme of surveillance'. This allowed authority to be exercised through the command of abstract knowledge and the communication of rules, formats, and technologies useful for administration'.[4] Knowledge is power: in times of peace, administrators seek knowledge that will enable them to run and fund the state; in times of unrest and war, spies enable those in charge to learn their enemies' intentions and smite them.

But this kind of centralized information collation served no more than the purposes of taxation, requisition and assessing of noble strengths. There was not the infrastructure, personnel, technology, governance or intention to micro-manage peasants' daily affairs. All that was expected was that they paid their tithes to the Church and their landlord, refrained from revolt and gave up some men for militia work now and again. Social and moral norms were instilled by family heads and village elders, enforced by the confessionals of the Church and supported by the casual social surveillance of small rural communities.

Not that heavy surveillance did not exist in the Middle Ages. Nicholas Brembre, the Lord Mayor of London in the 1380s, was a poor, paranoid grocery oligarch (ye olde Wal-Mart) who held on to office by rigging elections via intimidation, by preventing public gatherings, and by slandering his opponents while putting anyone suspected of making derogatory remarks about him under house arrest. London under his tyranny was a claustrophobic city where guild members and mercers forever feared spies and eavesdroppers.[5] He ended up beheaded for treason in 1388. In contrast – at least according to Shakespeare, whose plays are rife with spies and subterfuge – the legendary King Henry V's success at Agincourt was in part due to his sneaking about among his own men on the eve of battle to test their loyalty and to spread a little propaganda.[6]

The technology of migration surveillance was well established by the Middle Ages. Wax seals, stamps and watermarks, long used by bureaucrats across the world to authenticate documents, came into widespread use for travel documents, letters of safe conduct and missives borne by Europe's nobles, envoys and merchants as they roved the continent's city-states, principalities and kingdoms in the 13th century. Personal portraits were not reproduced in any form, not even as woodcuts, but the authorities instead relied primarily on words[7] for identification – sometimes just names or cursory physical descriptions, but often including descriptions of clothing, which provided the biggest clue to status in a socially immobile Europe. A circulated missive describing the wanted leader of a peasants' revolt in Breisgau, Germany, in 1517 talked of his white coat, black velvet lining, and the small silver arrow in his hat – a noble, no less, as most 'radicals' often are. From the late 14th century, letters describing known felons and outlaws were circulating between towns guarded by sentinels wearing civic insignia. Sometimes, stamped tokens or notes were issued for the poor to prove their means-tested entitlement to alms. By the 16th century, French and Swiss cantons sought ID to weed out army deserters, while travelers in northern Italy were required to carry certificates warranting their good health in times of plague – an early example of epidemic surveillance. Hence, function creep pervaded ID from its origins, from its use among the élite in diplomacy and business, to crime fighting, social services and healthcare.

The Spanish Inquisition

Such ID was also being used to control migration and enforce racial policies. By the 16th century, Spanish citizens were seeking leave to travel to the New World but, from the time of Philip II, they needed written proof, confirmed by their hometown governors, of their identity, appearance and any distinguishing marks, to prove they were not descendants of converted Jews, Muslims or heretics. The country's ruling nobles, having only recently wrested Iberia from Moorish control, joined up with the Catholic Church to seal their rule. Revitalizing a long-dormant

A brief history of surveillance

Papal Bull that sought to counter any 'perceived threat to national security from Jews, Muslims, and "all manner of heretics"', every cleric, noble, bureaucrat and burgher was bade to keep vigilant for heretics and the seditious, whose beliefs or acts threatened 'moral and civic well-being'.[8] A centralized Holy Office, supported by one of the most modern bureaucracies of its time, directed this Inquisition that viewed any recent converts to Catholicism as the most likely to be disloyal. Those suspected found themselves arrested and hauled before a court, with local records and interrogation establishing their name, trades, associates, studies, dwellings, travels, parentage and grandparentage. Their most recent confession could also be used in evidence, while their knowledge of the principal prayers or the Catechism was tested.[9] They could be tried for offenses ranging from petty blasphemous comments to doubting the immortality of the soul, but usually their guilt was assumed and their crimes corroborated by anonymous testimonies. A comment such as 'men are born and die, that's it,' suggested a secret Judaist, bad blood and an eternally disloyal heart. Spaniards suspected of Jewish or Muslim rituals had their lives plumbed by interrogators to see what predefined qualities these suspects might have that indicated disloyalty in the blood.

Having successfully eradicated the doubters of Rome, the remit of the Holy Office was then broadened to become a 'political policing force devoted to opposing the introduction of revolutionary and liberal ideas' or anyone else – Illuminists, witches, children – the Inquisitors could go at to keep busy and justify their existence. By the late 18th century, the Holy Office had begun to eat its own tail, turning Inquisitors' attentions increasingly inward on the Church's own monks and clerics, before snuffing itself out. But the Inquisition's flame still burned bright in the Spanish-dominated regions of South and Central

America. European disease did more to kill off the locals than Christian fervor, but it still left a labor deficit for the colonizers. So by the 17th century was beginning in earnest the Atlantic slave trade and the apocalyptic plunder of Africa's peoples.

From slavery to the Terror

The New World was built upon the prejudices of the Old World. In the North, slave passes were set up in the Virginia colony in 1642, specifically to identify indentured Irish servants and poor whites. The system was extended to cover native Americans entering the colony to trade, then to include the increasing numbers of imported slaves. In the landholdings of pre-Revolutionary America was born the surveillance infrastructure of colonial America. The slave master's inventories listed land, tools and animals along with people who were generally deprived of a surname as well as pay, education or religion. This helped to suppress any notions of individuality or humanity and kept slaves in line, but also frustrated their identification whenever they did rise up or run off.[10]

ID requirements were extended to slaves in Barbados after an insurrection there, and soon 'slave passes' became the norm for slaves moving between plantation living areas or to towns on their master's business. In the US South, slave patrols ranged the highways and were empowered to search homes for runaways, weapons or anything comprising a possible plot, and to whip any slave found without a pass. These passes were simple documents that some literate slaves could 'hack' and adjust for their own purposes. They were not at first suspected because, officially, all slaves were illiterate. Slave patrols, meanwhile, were not necessarily literate, and so could be fooled by a canny slave waving any old bit of paper.

The problem with this ID system, then, lay not in its technical fallibility, but rather in the over-riding and dangerous belief in the system's infallibility. So ever more details were added to the passes, proto-biometrics such as height, age, complexion, to scars on forehead, gaps in teeth, clothing, eyes, level of intelligence. Owners, meanwhile, were compelled to support the slave patrols via taxation.

The American Revolution of the 1770s offered liberation – but only to white men wanting to escape the remote rule of decadent British aristocrats. Still, it put fire in the empty bellies of French peasants and urbanites wrung thin by their own warmonger-ing, spendthrift aristocrats, and France's royals were bloodily deposed in 1789. But the leaders of France's New Order soon realized that those same masses of people who had brought them to power had done so by overturning centuries-old feudalism overnight and could therefore dispatch any young pretenders with far greater alacrity. Security depended on citizens' loyalty, and instilling schoolchildren with the grand ideals of national patriotism and allegiance to the state was the long game. So the Committee of Public Safety was set up to legislate and extend the New Order's centralized power and defend it from counter-revolutionaries, with a Law of Suspects used to hunt down those whose conduct, relations, words or writings showed them to be 'Partisans of tyranny, federalism and enemies of liberty', or had had patriotism certificates refused. Committees of Surveillance were set up in 1793 to draw up lists of suspects who could be dispatched to Revolutionary Tribunals and likely execution, as the state institution-alized violence against the people. A previous acquittal or a document of 'no occasion for indictment' was no protection from re-arrest.[11] By early 1794, job lots of suspects were being herded into the Paris Revolutionary Tribunal every day, the indictments read out *en masse*, then found summarily guilty and guillotined. Witnesses brought in to vouch for the accused were found guilty by association. Thousands were killed across the country until, in July 1794, the snake ate its own tail, and the architect of this Grande Terreur, Maximilien Robespierre, denounced one loyalist too many and got the chop. A legacy of the revolution would be the terms 'terrorists' and 'terrorism'. Though used in the modern era to identify violent disaffected individuals and to justify all manner of surveillance, these terms originated from the Revolutionary government's use of terror as a state tool to keep the masses loyal and obedient. France's Terror was inflicted even though the citizens were 'protected' by a new bill of rights and a constitution – paralleling later developments in the EU.

Prison and Panopticon

Before all the head-chopping, the English philosopher Jeremy Bentham traveled to France to seek comments on his new design of prison, the Panopticon. This was a cylindrical structure, with cells placed around the outer walls, all of which could be fully observed from a central viewing tower and listened in on by sound tubes.[12] Prisoners could be observed and heard continuously but very efficiently, requiring very low levels of staffing to maintain the surveillance. Of even greater importance, thought Bentham, was that the prisoners would assume they were being continuously watched at all times, and become acquiescent and obedient as a consequence. While largely moribund in Bentham's lifetime, the Panopticon has become central to the philosophy of surveillance, exemplifying the power and utility of design to enforce a regime of discipline. But the Panopticon's first purpose was actually industrial, being initially conceived by Jeremy's brother Samuel while working in Russia's steel, distilling and glass-making industries to solve the problem of keeping large numbers of workers under diligent observation and oversight. This dual-use nature of technology is a common feature in the surveillance field.

A brief history of surveillance

As the heads of France's aristocrats rolled, the wheels of Britain's Industrial Revolution turned. Burgeoning capitalist enterprises required labor, and so village populations – which had found their pastoral lives foreclosed as enclosure sealed off the common lands – were herded into the choking towns and cities. Their new lives were oriented around the fierce regulation and surveillance of their time demanded by the mass production of goods and materials. Violent action against the machines and enclosures, for example by the Luddites, provoked the British Home Office to set up spies to infiltrate and sabotage strikes and protest marches.

The tide of industrialization across Europe met a rising bow-wave of resistance, and governments, industrialists and landowners joined forces in arming militias to prevent the proles overthrowing them *à la* France. With the cross-continental revolutions of 1848 barely put down, surveillance systems became more structured and the militias and police forces of Europe's élites began in earnest to collaborate and co-operate in pooling data about radicals. By the end of the 19th century, all of Europe's interior ministries were exchanging information on real and supposed anarchists, terrorists and socialists.[13]

The secret service in the 20th century

By the turn of the 20th century, investigators for the first US centralized domestic intelligence unit, the Secret Service – set up in 1865 not to protect presidents but to protect the currency from counterfeiting – were in high demand by other government departments wanting to check up on tax fraud and track down major crooks. This worried the Legislature, one Congress member warning in 1908 that a 'general system of espionage is being conducted by the general government' (an uncanny parallel to the charges levied against the George W Bush administration a century later) – and the rise of 'black cabinets' (as clandestine as later off-sheet military 'black projects'). President Theodore Roosevelt retorted: 'There is no more foolish outcry than this against "spies" – only criminals need fear our detectives' (a precursor of the modern phrase 'nothing to hide, nothing to fear'). Still, the Legislature voted to limit the funding and loaning out of Secret Service agents, and a shortfall of investigators befell the government[14] – except at the Department of Justice. There, in 1909, Attorney-General Charles Bonaparte founded a small group of detectives, which within just two years would triple in size and be 'greatly broadened [in] its investigative authority', as it became the Federal Bureau of Investigation (FBI).[15]

In the same year, the UK set up its own Secret Service Bureau (the term 'bureau' apparently denoting a right and proper surveillance agency). The SSB – later known as MI5 when its existence was officially acknowledged – had its origins in 1903, when two good British chaps on a sailing holiday came across 'strange goings-on' in the North Sea involving the Imperial German Navy. Realizing they were watching the Hun prepare to invade England, they acted on their vigilance and botched the 'Boche' peril to King and country. Admittedly this was just Erskine Childers' swashbuckling Edwardian fiction, *The Riddle of the Sands*. But the real First Lord of the Admiralty, Lord Selborne, who read the book, reasoned that there was no way to tell if such goings-on were really happening, without spies to prove it, and set up the SSB.[16] Surveillance, then, can be less about what is, than about what might be – even when such fears are literally based on fiction.

Secret police in Russia and Germany

The Romanov royal dynasty in Russia was supported by the Ochrinka secret police, set up under Nicholas I in 1826 to counter the revolutionary ideas spreading across Europe. The Ochrinka's malevolence helped to fuel the terror and discontent of the masses, and the privations of the fantastic losses inflicted on Russia during the Great War proved radicalizing enough to spark the revolutions of 1917. As in revolutionary France, the Bolshevik leaders of Russia feared a counter-revolution and so aimed to instill fear in the masses and flush out the potentially disloyal, ends to which the Ochrinka, rebranded as the Cheka or NKVD, were directed under the Red Terror of 1918 and beyond. Disloyalty could be deduced not from evidence of counter-revolutionary comments or acts, but by profiling citizens' status in society, with interrogators to ask which class suspects belonged to, and what was their background, education and profession. It was a murderous irony that the Cheka's boss, Felix Dzerzhinsky, was an aristocrat-turned-communist, but the rules are different for those in power.

Meanwhile, the terrified royalists, capitalists, democrats and dictators beyond Russia launched their own White Terror to flush out communists, particularly in eastern European states under the aegis of fascist regimes. But in 1930s Germany it was Jews, Romanies and dissidents as well as communists that the Nazi state sought to sniff out by way of the Gestapo. The German secret police force's methods of supervision and repression were, ironically, closely modeled on those of its Bolshevik enemy, the USSR. Gestapo chief Heinrich Müller was a 'close and devoted student of Soviet methods' and was impressed by the NKVD's efficiency, the effect of which was to isolate people by making it impossible for them to trust each other. All German police were co-opted for Gestapo work, and every labor group had a Gestapo representative so as to minimize the number and scale of industrial disputes. This made Nazi Germany extremely attractive to outside investors, particularly US firms such as Ford, Coca-Cola and IBM.

While the Gestapo tapped phones and intercepted mail, it was its army of informers, willing to plumb any depth of mundanity, that gave the force its psychological potency, down to apartment-block concierges reporting on the comings and goings of every tenant. These volunteers would often denounce people less out of political fervor than to ingratiate themselves with the authorities.[17] As the Russians had discovered, the voluntary informer system created a general climate of unease. While the information gleaned was often worthless, it did convey to the population the impression of police omniscience or chilled them with the knowledge that a spy was in their midst.[18] All citizens were free to denounce one another for criminal, social, political, racial or sexual offenses and comments; unsuitable spouses could be 'dumped' by denunciation. The hasty look to right and left before making a risqué comment in public became the giveaway 'German glance'.

For the golden children of the Third Reich, this became the social norm. From 1933 onwards, it was compulsory for parents to enroll their children in the Hitler Youth or League of German Girls on pain of fines, prison and losing their children. Children were taught that their loyalty to their parents should be relatively unimportant. They should be loyal first to the Führer and the state, then to their friends. They were free to denounce any child or adult for making derisory comments about Hitler, having Jewish friends or being unpatriotic (children were free to beat any Jew they met). The family atmosphere was often poisoned, and parents were often required to become cautious in front of their children.

While the Nazi war machine eventually lashed out and consumed tens of millions of lives in the European theater of World War Two, within its own expanded territories it would burn some six million undesirables, including the Jews, the disabled, homosexuals and Romanies, traced by their home state's bureaucracies, ID'd by colored stars, shipped off for slave labor or extermination in concentration camps where punchcard machines supplied by IBM sorted and sifted them by nationality, 'crime', work skills or type of death.

Surveillance in the Soviet bloc

The Soviet Communist Pioneer League movements were equally aggressive. The takeover of eastern Europe by the Soviet Union in 1945 only expanded Moscow's totalitarianism from the Pacific Coast and borders with India and Iran up to the Swiss Alps. This empire was metaphorically supported on columns of stacked files, and the slave labor in its Gulags contributed much to the Soviet economy. According to the theorist Maria Los: 'If fear can be construed as an inherent condition of totalitarian domination, the file may be its most recognizable symbolic prop.'[19]

In the east European Soviet empire, fear was internalized as people sought to be as normal and conformist as possible, mentally closing out 'danger' subjects when talking to strangers in case a criticism could lead to a new black mark in their secret file, cursing them and their children. This 'taboo-mentality' became innate, as is shown by the Behrend family in Anna Funder's book *Stasiland*. This East German family were not dissidents, churchgoers, environmentalists; they had no run-ins with the state. They were just 'an ordinary family'. But from the minute they woke up they knew what could be said at home (most things up to a point) and outside the home (very little). Many people withdrew into what they called 'internal emigration'. They sheltered their secret inner lives in an attempt to keep something of themselves from the authorities.[20] The state's 'permanent residency' in people's minds led to 'psychic disrepair on a massive scale – paranoia, clinical depression, chronic internalized anger and learned helplessness'.

By the time the Berlin Wall fell in 1989, the Stasi – the East German secret police – had 97,000 employees and over 173,000 informers among a population of 17 million. This was one for every 63 people, compared with Stalin's USSR, which had one KGB agent for every 5,830 people, and Hitler's Third Reich, which had one Gestapo agent for every 2,000 people. If part-time informers were included, moreover, the East Germans had one agent or informer for every 6.5 people. The paranoia of the man leading the Stasi helped fire this growth: 'Everywhere Mielke found opposition he found enemies, and the more enemies he found the more staff and informers he hired to quell them.'[21]

J Edgar Hoover's FBI

When the US Federal Bureau of Investigation (FBI) was directed to battle Nazi sympathizers and communists, gangsters and Ku Klux Klan in the 1930s, there was at least some point to their activities. But the FBI boss J Edgar Hoover was a man of unfathomable ambition and malevolence, and showed how even in a democracy, surveillance could be viciously abused to serve one man's purposes. Hoover transformed the FBI into his own anti-democratic weapon, wielding hidden power by blackmail and smear.

As President Truman warned in 1947: 'All Congressmen and Senators are afraid of Hoover... Edgar Hoover's organization would make a good start towards a citizen spy system. If I can prevent it, there'll be no NKVD or Gestapo in this country.' But it was Truman who, that same year, created the 'Federal Employees Loyalty Program' that sacked and blacklisted any government employee considered 'unAmerican'. Senator Joe McCarthy's House of UnAmerican Activities Committee took up this Red Scare baton, the Committee's public interrogations and denunciations ruining thousands of careers and causing numerous suicides. Hoover's FBI helped fabricate the evidence.

Stalin's power rested on people's terror of the KGB, yet Hoover made the American people overlook the FBI's encroaching threat to their freedom by having his G-Men glamorized through gushing articles placed in the press, through heroic radio programs, films and later TV shows, and by merchandising the G-Men brand on toy guns, badges and children's pajamas.[22] Behind this brilliant PR were programs like the Counter Intelligence program (COINTELPRO), which expanded the Fed's operational tactics from infiltration and informer networks to illegal wire-tapping, break-ins, planting of false evidence, blackmailing and smears. Among the targets were civil rights groups, women rights groups, peace groups, environmentalists, Nation of Islam members and black nationalists, and agents went beyond infiltration to inciting groups to commit criminal acts.[23] Much energy was spent, for example, smearing Martin Luther King Jr as a dangerous, Moscow-minded radical. Lie-filled dossiers about King's 'personal conduct' were sent to Sweden to guard against his winning the Nobel Peace Prize and in the hope of sinking King into depression and obscurity. John Lennon and Jane Fonda were among the most prominent targets of Hoover's paranoia but tens of thousands of ordinary Americans and outsiders were also targeted.

Hoover ran the Feds from 1924 until his death in 1972, with the apparently consistent support of Congress, because no-one could fire him. As President Nixon fumed: 'He had files on everybody, Goddamnit.'[24]

Cold War espionage
The search for the enemy within was the home front for the truly global Cold War, in which the Capitalist

West and Communist East fought their battles under-cover. Among the threats to the Western powers was the danger that they would lose their supplies of cheap raw materials from former colonies and their neighbors. Hence the US Central Intelligence Agency (CIA) led the Western world's work in bolstering the surveillance and policing capabilities of Third World states, often taking up the slack left by departing European colonial powers.

The CIA and MI6 assassinated Iranian democracy in 1953 when they brought down elected prime minister Mohammed Mossadeq, whose crime was to have nationalized the country's oil, removing it from BP's ownership. Mossadeq was replaced by the autocratic rule of the Shah, kept in power by Persia's first modern, effective and terrifying secret police, SAVAK, which was trained by the CIA and the Israeli secret service, MOSSAD.[25] With 5,000 core staff supported by 50,000 part-timers, SAVAK censored all publications and screened all government job applicants. Anyone considered a dissident – communists, playwrights, poets, teachers – was in danger of being tracked down, imprisoned, tortured with sleep deprivation, by having their fingernails pulled out, or worse. SAVAK had an international wing to track down opponents abroad. Its activities certainly helped fuel the rage required for Ayatollah Khomeini's overthrow of the corrupt Shah in 1979, but SAVAK, having failed to prevent the revolution, benefited in the aftermath, being given a fundamentalist make-over; it proved all the more effective in finding those disloyal to Allah as well as to the state.

In 1980 the West sought to bring down Khomeini by covertly backing the invasion of Iran by the dictator of neighboring Iraq. Saddam Hussein's own tortuous ascent to power involved CIA-backed coups, while his tenure rested on the Mukhabarat secret police, as well schooled in suppression, torture and murder as

SAVAK. Similarly, Egypt's secret police were founded by the British, and then trained by the CIA in torture methods such as rubbing prisoners with animal fat and setting dogs on them.[26]

Washington brought down Chile's elected socialist president Salvador Allende first by covert sanctions and financial machinations that throttled the Chilean economy, then by having the CIA back General Augusto Pinochet's coup in 1973, in the course of which Allende was murdered. The newly founded Direccion de Inteligencia Nacional secret police closed newspapers, detained, tortured and disappeared over 3,000 'radicals' – politicos, journalists, academics, poets, trade unionists, teachers, students and friends – who 'threatened' the junta under its unceasing 'state of emergency'. In next-door Argentina, the intelligence services' 'dirty war' led to the disappearance of at least 9,000 individuals considered to be threats to the military dictatorship.

Watergate and the dark underworld of espionage

By now, Americans were looking to Washington for the ultimate in surveillance skulduggery. In 1974, Richard Nixon became the first US President ever to resign, bringing himself down with his own Oval Office tape-recording system that recorded his elephantine efforts to cover up the Watergate scandal, itself a failed attempt by ex-CIA crooks to burgle and bug the Democrats' Watergate office. Watergate goaded a shocked US Senate, no longer in the shadow of Hoover's menace, to plumb the depths of the security services' own shenanigans against US citizens, and the Church and Rockefeller committees of the mid-1970s scratched the surface of a very dark underworld of American espionage.

While Americans were shocked by the exposure of plots like that against Chile's President Allende, it was the domestic US surveillance revelations that were most shocking, among them operations such as COINTELPRO, CHAOS and MINARET. CHAOS involved the National Security Agency (NSA) handing the CIA 1,100 pages of data on apparent foreign influences of radical groups. From 1967 to 1973, MINARET had the NSA intercept the calls and cables of 1,680 US citizens and 5,925 foreigners across 1,000 groups deemed 'suspicious' by the FBI, CIA and the Defense Intelligence Agency, from drug traffickers to anti-war groups. These were projects of such dubious legality that the Attorney-General halted them in 1973.

Hitherto, the public and most of the Senate had not even known the NSA existed. The NSA had grown out of a tiny clandestine code-breaking and interception agency, the Black Chamber, set up during World War One, through which all the telegrams sent within and via the US were passed, as censorship laws dictated. The end of the war brought the need for censorship to a close – so the Black Chamber cut a secret deal with Western Union, among others, to keep receiving the telegrams. Secretary of State Henry Stimpson closed the Chamber in 1929, stating 'Gentlemen do not read each other's mail', but when Secretary of War in 1941 he realized the need to do so and reopened the Chamber as the SSA, again making deals with Western Union and friends that continued post-World War Two.

Bolstered by the armed services' signal intelligence units, the SSA became the National Security Agency in 1952 – Congress was not even told – and at the NSA's offices in Fort Meade, Maryland, sat the US's first supercomputer, Harvest, processing copies of the computerized tapes of all telegram traffic entering, exiting and traversing the US. These tapes were handed over to agents in New York back alleys, or, as at AT&T, given their own 'secret room'.[27] Appalled that private firms would so willingly snoop on the public, the American Civil Liberties Union in 1975 filed a half-billion dollar lawsuit against the NSA and CIA, RCA Global Communications, ITT World Communications, Western Union, and American Cable & Radio Corp.[28] Meanwhile the Legislature turned its wrath on the federal eavesdropping on US citizens, violating the Fourth Amendment, and passed the 1978 Foreign Intelligence Surveillance Act (FISA), creating judicial and congressional oversight of governmental covert surveillance and requiring a court order to spy on US citizens. Although flawed and later circumvented, FISA was a seminal moment in the reawakening of Americans' consciousness about government surveillance.

Globalization and telecoms

Still, FISA pretty much designated foreigners as fair game for the NSA, which had been its main function since its inception anyway – except that now it had the technology of global telecoms to work with. The NSA was working globally with a cabal of White Anglo Saxon Protestant (WASP) states – the UK, Canada, Australia and New Zealand – to tap the burgeoning global telecommunications networks. During World War Two, the US and UK codified their sharing of intelligence and intercepts about the Axis powers under the 1943 BRUSA agreement. In 1947, this arrangement expanded into the Cold War with the Commonwealth SIGINT (Signal Intelligence) Organization, involving Canada, Australia and New Zealand in the hosting of listening posts across the dying British Empire's dominions and the brash new US empire. This global communications network, with outposts on land, at sea, in air and space, intercepting every phone call, email, fax, telex or message sent by radio, television, microwave, cellular, satellite or fibre-optic communications, would be called ECHELON. All the intelligence is fed through supercomputers for keywords, and systems for converting speech into text. VOICECAST recognizes individuals' speech patterns and automatically records what they say, with programs like MAGISTRAND and PATHFINDER sifting the text for keywords that are flagged. The text is then pushed to humintel (human intelligence operatives) for further analysis.

Exemplifying how enemies can be allies at one and the same time, China was monitored, until 1997, from Hong Kong, but as Sino-US relations were more stable than Sino-Soviet relations, under Project P415, Chinese army staff trained in California to use ECHELON systems with two US-Chinese outposts in Xinjiang province.[29] Since then China's hegemonic threat has been more commercial than communist. Spying on foreign companies has become one of ECHELON's activities simply by redefining 'national security' to include corporate interests in a globalized world.[30]

Although microwave or satellite communications suffer time delays and interference, they are open for anyone to decrypt and monitor. Communication cables, if they are to be accessed, require the co-operation of the company that controls them.[31] But if the corporate world stood to gain from spying, they might co-operate instead of having to be co-opted. ECHELON was bound to do more than simply pay for itself in a world united by the concept of profit. But those who celebrate FISA's victory against state surveillance and invasions of privacy ain't seen nothing yet compared to the efforts of banks and private firms to annex every atom of data.

Finance, widgets and dataveillance

Communism offered a centralized state telling everyone how to think and behave, and using surveillance to force individuals into succumbing to the needs of the collective. The 'free' West preferred to allow private business to observe what individuals thought and direct their resources to meet individuals' wants by gauging what collective trends, based on aggregated data, suggested. Western governments, meanwhile, continued to direct resources based on the state providing where the market 'failed'. Both the private and public sectors required extensive 'surveillance' in varying forms to function, although more for the provision of services like health and education and the welfare of benefits and social services than for outright coercion.

By the 1980s, right-wingers were dismantling the meddling state so as to 'liberate the private sector' and deliver cheap debt-based prosperity for all – the hidden cost being people's loss of control of data about them. The arrival of cheap mass computing power allowed for the mass retention and rapid sifting and dissemination of people's personal data, creating what Professor Roger A Clarke would call 'dataveillance' – Western societies not governed by one Big Brother but by 1,000 little ones. This computer power enabled the kind of personalized, targeted financing that blossomed in the wake of the deregulation of the US and UK financial sectors. Private debt-propelled spending would fill the economic void left by rustbelt industries and rolled-up state spending, with the new employees of the booming finance-service industries spending by using new credit cards in new shopping malls built on industrial wastelands.

At the center of the debt boom were the banks, converting their depositors' reserves into multiples of interest-bearing loans to millions more people than ever before. Banks function by accounting for their deposits and loans, but they must also assess who is worth lending to and how credit-worthy they are, based on a borrower's income, assets, previous credit histories and other debts – in other words, by assessing what risk the borrower poses. Dataveillance computing power made it possible for billions of dollars to be loaned to tens of millions of previously excluded people and enabled banks, insurers and other financial services to grade and police the debtor's risk by crunching their personal and financial data. Technology enabled this to be done at any distance, remotely, but also anonymously. Globalization required the sifting and gauging of the credit status of billions of anonymous people while at the same time the normal modes of trust based on face-to-face interaction and small-world norms became redundant.

Countries are also subject to risk classification, with firms like Fitch Ratings and Standard & Poor giving school-report-like credit gradings of B, B-, CCC+. CCC means a country is 'currently vulnerable and dependent on favorable business, financial and economic conditions to meet financial commitments'. When sovereign states default on debt, geopolitical instability, social unrest and even war may arise – or, worse, investors do not get a return.

Risk can be judged wrongly, as when the global banking collapse of 2008 was traced back to the domino of debt emanating from the US sub-prime loans crisis. Here, the poorest of the poor, the biggest credit risks, had more debt sold to them then they could ever repay, while banks bought and sold reconstituted debts to one another in practices palpably not held to the same level of scrutiny as countries, consumers and citizens.

Marketing and pseudo-science
The origins of mass marketing in the UK go back to 1937, when Information Minister Duff Cooper set up the Mass Observation social research organization to carry out an 'anthropology' of the British. Clipboards in hand, people in mackintoshes stood on high streets, attended public meetings and sports events, and noted down everything people wore, bought, talked about

and read in the newspapers. Meanwhile, thousands of recruited diarists nationwide sent in regular material to the Mass Observation HQ, commenting not only on their own lives but those of their families, neighbors and friends. As Britain entered World War Two, people began to resent what was increasingly perceived as a gross invasion of privacy carried out by the Mass Observation workers – or, as they became known, Cooper's Snoopers.[32] But Mass Observation was less interested in noting what individuals thought than in shaping what the masses thought, and its data helped produce very effective army recruitment and propaganda campaigns for the government's war effort.

Based on this military success, Mass Observation methods were refined for use during Britain's 1950s consumer boom. Market research of 25,000 people and their opinions on everything from baked beans to TV programs, produced data used by the British Market Research Bureau to gauge consumer sentiment. The data has also been used to grade and stratify society, incorporating all facets of people's class, gender and status in society, and this has developed into a worldwide pseudo-science of astonishing complexity.

One US firm, Claritas, redacts society into 15 different groups, subgroups and mind-blowing nicknames. This consumer pyramid, as they see it, runs from the Elite Suburbs (Blue Blood Estates, Winner's Circle, Executive Suites, Pools & Patios, Kids & Cul-de-Sacs) through Urban Cores (Single City Blues, Hispanic Mix) and the Working Towns (Golden Ponds, Norma Rae-ville, Mines and Mills) to Rustic Living (Rustic Elders, Scrub Pine Flats, Hard Scrabble…).

Individual targeting requires name, date of birth, social security number, marital status, level of solvency and credit worthiness, income, race, height, weight, body mass index, phone number, job, and education.

But the list does not stop there: magazine subscriptions, music and book preferences, membership of clubs or social groups, diet, allergies, incontinence, bad eyesight; all these things are of interest to a marketer needing to ensure that junk mail or email hits the spot.

In the US, the big gun behind this is the Direct Marketing Association, its Direct Media List Showcase highlighting sub-categories such as, for example, Catholics who subscribe to *Newsweek* magazine. Ethnic and religious profiling is also used by Dr Leonard's Healthcare Lifelines, or by Affluent America, which punts at 'millionaires, multi-millionaires and billionaires... the top five per cent of American families'.[33] Names mean leads mean money. A thousand names is worth $65, and even refusal to participate is profitable, since those opting out must pay $5 to the Direct Marketing Association then wait five years for their data to be removed.

The move towards a cashless society

Again, new technology has enabled this minute-by-minute detailing of everyone's every purchase, with anonymous cash supplanted by audit-trailing credit and debit cards and internet shopping. Shopping is being made faster and more convenient with swipe-the-lot 'tap and pay' cards, like Texas Instruments and American Express's ExpressPay system, MasterCard's PayPass or Halifax's Visa payWave. Cards are also now incorporating travel card functions like Oyster or MoLo Reward's Radio Frequency Identifier-charged supermarket loyalty cards so customers can get coupons and points at a contactless point-of-sale.[34]

Unlike cash, every dollar within these electronic systems is accountable and taxable. This allows state coffers to fill without the public being directly taxed more, while banks can apply charges for every transaction made through their systems.[35] Workers who have hitherto been paid in cash are therefore switched to being paid via bank accounts and charged for the privilege of occasional reminders and high-interest loans being hawked at them. Recipients of state benefits or pensions who previously cashed their checks must now funnel them through their bank accounts enabling banks to claim fatter reserves and lend more.

The new electronic systems mean that insurers can better judge personal risk premiums while manufacturers and service sellers can better target – and discard – customers. Checks are increasingly being rendered obsolete or simply refused, and people are increasingly required to pay utility bills by direct debit. This does remove hassle but it hands control of payment from the payer to the payee, who may charge too much and tip the payer into overdraft and a penalty payment from their bank. Inevitably it is those with the lowest income (and the highest risk) who incur such charges most often as well as falling victim to loans with the highest interest payments.

Predictions of the death of cash have long been exaggerated. But there is no doubt that we are moving towards a cashless society because of the advantage of electronic transactions to private companies of all kinds. 'All credit or debit-related purchases already generate monitorable and searchable real-time information; but more and more transactions will be of this kind as we move towards a cashless society...' – so noted mysterious think-tank the Future Group in a paper for the European Commission.[36] Someone who avoids such transactions – who does not use a credit card, does not drive and does not own a home, perhaps – is effectively a mystery to the private sector compared with a 'normal' card-wielding person and therefore something of a risk.[37]

Yet the new electronic world of finance, telecoms and credit transfers carries its own huge risks. Criminals and terrorists are able to orchestrate their plots from anywhere in the world by globalized means. And as the 21st century made its debut, the threats of global terrorism and migration were bombed onto the world's consciousness by 9/11 – and a globalized governmental response of surveillance followed in its train.

1 Job 34 21-22. 2 Qur'an 89.14. 3 Richard fitzNigel, writing c. 1179. 4 Maurice Punch, Richard Victor Ericson & Kevin D Haggerty, *Policing the Risk Society*, University of Toronto Press, 1997. 5 Marion Turner, *Chaucerian conflict: languages of antagonism in late fourteenth-century London*, OUP, 2007. 6 *Henry V*, Act IV, Scene 1. 7 Valentin Groebner, *Identification, Deception and Surveillance in Early Modern Europe*, Zone Books, 2007. 8 Sherene Razack, *Casting Out*, University of Toronto Press, 2008. 9 Joseph Perez, *The Spanish Inquisition*, Yale University Press, 2007. 10 Christian Parenti, *The Soft Cage*, Basic Books, 2003. 11 Philip G Dwyer, Peter McPhee (eds), *The French Revolution and Napoleon: A sourcebook*, Routledge 2002. 12 Catherine Pease-Watson, (2003) 'Bentham's Panopticon and Dumont's Panoptique', *Journal of Bentham Studies*, 6, 2003. 13 Garry Kinsman, Dieter Buse, Mercedes Steedman (eds), *Whose National Security?* Between the Lines, 2000. 14 John F Fox PhD thesis, July 2003. 15 www.fbi.gov/libref/historic/history/artspies/artspies.htm 16 www.guardian.co.uk/uk/2009/jan/07/counter-espionage-british-history 17 George Victor, *Hitler: the pathology of evil*, Brassey's, 1998. 18 Edward Crankshaw, *Gestapo*, Panther, 1960. 19 Anna Los, Maria Los, in David Lyon (ed), *Theorizing Surveillance – the panopticon and beyond*, Willan Publishing, 2006. 20 Anna Funder, *Stasiland*, Granta, 2003. 21 Henry Porter 'The limits of liberty – we are all suspects now', www.henry-porter.com 22 Anthony Summers, *The Secret Life of J Edgar Hoover*, Orion, 1993. 23 www.trackedinamerica.org 24 John Parker, *Total Surveillance*, Piatkus, 2000. 25 NR Keddie and MJ Gasiorowski (eds), *Neither East Nor West. Iran, the United States, and the Soviet Union*, New Haven, 1990. 26 Adam Curtis, *The Power of Nightmares* episode 2, BBC TV, 2004. 27 James Bamford, *Body of Secrets* (Doubleday 2001)& Chris Calabrese Program Counsel of the ACLU Technology and Liberty Project. 28 James Bamford, 'NSA: Inside the Puzzle Palace', *Time*, 10 Nov 1975. 29 Duncan Campbell, *New Statesman*, 12 Aug 1988. 30 Keith Laidler, *Surveillance Unlimited*, Icon, 2008. 31 James Bamford, Confronting the Surveillance Society forum, www.youtube.com/watch?v=VojZOaJ6gpk 32 Ben Wilson, *What Price Liberty*, Faber, 2009. 33 Privacy and Consumer Profiling, Electronic Privacy Information Centre http://epic.org/privacy/profiling/default.html 34 Jonathan Collins, 'RFID Speeds Sorting of Packages', 6 Aug 2003, www.rfidjournal.com/article/view/526 35 Glenn Newman, 'A Cashless Economy Would Make Larger Tax Cuts Possible, *New York Times*, 5 Nov 1994. 36 Tony Bunyan, *The Shape of Things to Come*, Spokesman, 2009. 37 see footnote 32.

3 The death of privacy

Fear of terrorism and technological advance are together bringing about a greater intrusion by governments, security forces and corporations into the privacy of individuals than has ever been known before. And still there is the hunger for more knowledge, more intrusion, more control. Where will it end?

IN THE WORLD of the 21st century, globalization and technology allow consumers to gain instant credit from afar and to buy goods made even further afield. Consumer goods are purchased over the monitorable internet by auditable credit cards and tracked across the globe by Radio Frequency Identification (RFID) chips. These RFID chips are also being inserted into the passports of the migrating millions. And all of this activity can be monitored in real time.

Governments worldwide, aided and abetted by private firms, have also been seeking to deal with the globalized problems of criminal and terrorist activities. What the events of 11 September 2001 did was demolish any restraints – political, moral or legal – on governments and agencies seeking to identify potential threats. Anyone who was suspected could, courtesy of technology, be searched.

The response of the US neo-conservatives who had just been installed as the masters of the 'free world' was to make a bid to turn the US into a police state almost overnight. The first assault on US privacy and liberty was the USA Patriot Act, passed through the Senate by a majority of 98 to 1 just six weeks after 9/11. Many senators later confessed that they had never read the Act, but of course they were not supposed to do so – the Act was a 300-page tome of hideous complexity that had actually been prepared long before 9/11.

From the Patriot Act would arise a bonanza of dubious databases and short-lived schemes. Most notable for its hubris was the Pentagon's Total Information Awareness (TIA) program, developed at the Defense Advance Research Projects Agency under the auspices of disgraced Admiral John Poindexter, of Iran-Contra infamy. The TIA's goal was to 'determine the feasibility of searching vast quantities of data to determine links and patterns indicative of terrorist activities'. In order to detect and pre-empt any terrorist anywhere, everybody was under suspicion and every database was to be searched[1] – which was ironic, because the most specific terrorist target was al-Qaeda, which translates as 'the list' or 'the database', the name given by US agents to Osama bin Laden's loose network of affiliates in the 1990s.

The real-time transactions now pivotal to modernity's functioning had created a transaction space crossed by trails that TIA could follow up, explained program manager Ted Senator in 2002: 'I had to arrange for airline tickets and hotel reservations and airport transportation. I sent emails to colleagues and to friends to co-ordinate schedules. I had to co-ordinate schedules with my wife and children. I checked airline reservation websites for flight options. I registered. And I must have sent and received innumerable emails with various drafts of this talk.'

Finance-industry risk gradings would be adapted for terrorism and fraud detection techniques used to seek 'outliers' – individuals whose behavior was unusual according to some statistical measure. But the most dangerous adversaries were presumed to be 'inliers', those 'who most successfully disguise their individual transactions to appear normal, reasonable, and legitimate'. In other words, being an upstanding, law-abiding citizen warranted greater suspicion. It was envisaged that the TIA would cover the totality of an individual's affairs – financial, education, travel, medical, veterinary, housing, critical resources, communications – as well as those of family members, neighbors and business associates. TIA would tap worldwide databases as if they were 'one centralized database' to identify potential terrorists and their supporters. Which bytes of data would be relevant in proving that could not be known at the outset, so every byte of everyone's data needed sifting, privacy being the last vestige of the guilty.

Meanwhile, the Federal Emergency Management Agency was exhorting truckers, train conductors, postal workers, plumbers and others 'well positioned' to interact routinely with commuters or householders to report any suspicious activity to the Terrorist Information and Prevention System – TIPS. A million workers were to be drafted into the pilot phase of this Citizens' Corps.

Not even 9/11 could cow people into accepting these programs, and TIA and TIPS were killed off[2] – however, their spores were released. Out of TIPs grew Marine Watch, where fishing boats were to report anyone carrying the wrong-looking kit, and Community Anti-Terrorism training, which expanded Neighborhood Watch from preventing burglaries and cycling on pavements, to stopping terrorist attacks on prize flower beds, staffed by local Block Watchers and Block Captains. Meanwhile, Real Estate Watch would employ estate agents, those arbiters of truth, as spies. From the TIA's corpse would wriggle a thousand 'Little Brothers', like the Multistate Anti-Terrorism Information Exchange – the MATRIX – a state-level operation that appeared in states, including Connecticut, Florida and Utah, yet was federally funded by the Departments of Justice and Homeland Security. The MATRIX had the same breadth of database trawling as TIA, compiling and sharing dossiers on individuals for police or agents to find anomalies indicating terrorist or criminal proclivity.

Follow the money

Such programs were, however, a carpet-bomb approach. The key to combating crime and terrorism didn't just involve banks' logarithms of risk, it involved following the money. The post-Watergate push for privacy saw personal banking receive Fourth Amendment protection under the 1978 Right to Financial Privacy Act. The FBI successfully lobbied Congress to amend the Act so that, based on 'specific and articulable facts', agents could get a National Security Letter (NSL) off an FBI director allowing them to access the transactions of foreign nationals or their associates; these Letters would then double as search warrants and gagging orders. The Patriot Act further watered down the foreign connection and 'articulable' suspicions to anything 'relevant to an authorized investigation to protect against international terrorism or clandestine intelligence activities', while FBI field offices could issue NSLs to access any American's financial and communication records. Whereas 8,500 NSLs were issued in 2000 for foreign nationals' records, by 2004 the tally was 56,507, mostly relating to US citizens, and Feds were accessing entire databases, including the mainframe of Connecticut's 26 independently operated public libraries. This led librarians to co-operate with the American Civil Liberties Union in suing the government under the First and Fourth Amendments, with the NSLs deemed unconstitutional. Still, between 2003 and 2005, 150,000 NSLs were issued, riddled with thousands of breaches of policy and regulation, based on administrative carelessness, confusion, bad training and oversight.[3]

At an international level, global worries about money laundering and the financing of terrorism had in 1989 led the G7, supported by Europe, to set up the Financial Action Task Force on Money Laundering (FATF), an inter-governmental body devoted to getting banks to identify their customers and keep good records. FATF's work as a 'policy-making' body generating 'the necessary political will' for international co-operation in fighting the financing of terrorism has been bolstered by conventions like the UN's 1999 International Convention for the Suppression of the Financing of Terrorism. This seeks better oversight of assets of 'every kind, whether tangible or intangible, movable or immovable, however acquired' and the legal documentation and transparent accounting of every penny, bond and security. Today, FATF's 34 core members and sub-groups work kid-gloved to instill transparency into the workings of financial institutions that don't appreciate the irony of being screened for 'risk', nor the loss of confidentiality that reduces people's incentive to bank with them, money-launderers or bombers though they may be.

Niceties like these take too long, however, especially when there exists an entity like the Brussels-based Society for Worldwide Interbank Financial Telecommunication (SWIFT – with over 8,300 banking organizations and corporate customers in 208 countries by 2009), which handles much of the world's bank and business transactions and messaging. Since the 1990s, US investigators had been seeking access to SWIFT and had been denied by banks and governments on grounds of privacy and confidentiality. 9/11 crashed such concerns to the ground, with President Bush's Terrorist Surveillance Program invoking the International Emergency Economic Powers Act so that the CIA or US Treasury could 'investigate, regulate or prohibit' any foreign financial transaction linked to 'an unusual and extraordinary threat'. SWIFT's data was to be swiftly subpoenaed, if not directly accessed, with no warrants required.[4]

The story broke in mid 2006, to a flurry of international consternation about the impact of US unilateralism, and a Belgian parliamentary commission shortly concluded that SWIFT, and the US branch of Dutch Rabobank, had for years 'secretly and systematically transferred massive amounts of personal data for surveillance without effective and clear legal basis and independent controls in line with Belgian and European law'. Amazingly, however, the commission concluded this did not mean there should be legal repercussions for SWIFT. And so, amid the clamor of condemnation from the EU's Privacy Commissioners, the European Parliament and the Swiss (big on banking), the European Union resolved only that EU banks should tell customers that SWIFT was handing their data to the US.[5]

As for balancing the needs of privacy and security, SWIFT boss Francis Vanbever blithely told the European Parliament that the EU should 'have talks' with the US, which the EU's foreign ministers ultimately did.[6] They did so without the European Parliament, despite the EU Council having received legal advice that the Parliament was legally obliged to be involved. As one EU official explained: 'The Council often follows the opinion of its legal services, but not always.'[7] European law, it seems, can be bent to fit US security demands: the eventual agreement codified full US access to Europe's banking affairs. The European Parliament was now pressured to 'fast-track' the agreement, despite its leaving citizens with questionable redress over their data protection.

The US listens in

Telecommunications, particularly the internet, provided global reach for free speech, and agencies therefore sought to put them under surveillance – 9/11 was a major impetus to and excuse for this effort, but was not the origin. By the early 1990s, the digitalization

The death of privacy

US Wiretapping 1979-2009*

The total number of Federal or State wiretaps on US citizens authorized
has consistently increased over the last three decades. Over the whole
period, only 12 requests for wiretaps were denied.

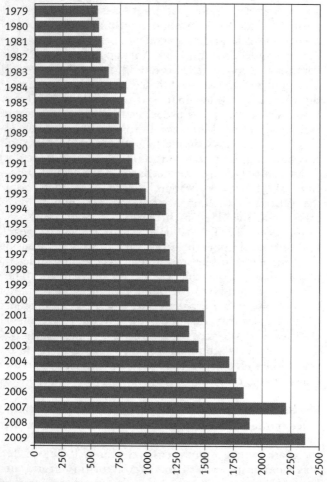

*Data on 1986 and 1987 is missing

Source: Electronic Privacy
Information Center

of telephone networks under way across the US was making wiretapping increasingly problematic, as the telecom companies' hardware and software mismatched with the secret agencies' bugging kits. So Congress was urged to pass the 1994 Communications Assistance for Law Enforcement Act, compelling telecoms to build and update digital networks to FBI specifications and wiretap kit compatibility, so as to ensure easy eavesdropping.[8] The cost of compliance would be borne by the companies, or rather by their customers, who would unknowingly be subsidizing another advance in the surveillance state. And so they did, with the Act amended to cover telephone service systems (Voice over Internet Protocol) and instant messaging as telephoning through internet servers and broadband providers grew apace. Developing systems with inbuilt access points for external tapping is dangerous, as hackers as well as the agencies can home in on them. These taps could be just left 'on', with or without any authorization.[9]

Just weeks after 9/11, classified Presidential Authorizations allowed the NSA and others to mine any seam of data they saw, whether the information ore was the quality of uranium or that of Play-doh.[10] The main aim was to intercept communications going in and out of the US if any party were suspected of terrorism, but this warrantless wiretapping based on suspicion alone directly conflicted with the FISA and the Fourth Amendment. Not that anyone knew about this until it was exposed in 2005, whereupon the White House justified the wiretapping by saying it was integral to the President's Surveillance Program. The FISA court had approved the President's Surveillance Program and, amid myriad court suits and rows, the wiretapping trundled on.

In 2007 the American Civil Liberties Union sued the NSA on suspicion that it was being bugged, but the case was thrown out by the court, which said suspicions were not proof, and any 'proof' would in any case be a state secret. The same fate awaited the Al-Haramain Islamic Foundation's suit against AT&T for its alleged complicity in the NSA's antics (the NSA was alleged to have started its wiretapping so quickly because the plan was hatched, and telecom firms co-opted for involvement, months before 9/11[11]). In 2007, the Democrat-controlled Legislature passed the Protect America Act, making all foreign-related communications passing through US networks fair game for warrantless surveillance, and granting immunity to participating companies[12] – an immunity which President Obama's Attorney-General later upheld in the face of a suit from the Electronic Frontier Foundation.[13]

Since the early 2000s, agencies had been tracking people through their cellphones, not just by triangulating their reception between antennae or inbuilt GPS, but by turning cellphones into what the US Department of Commerce called a 'microphone and transmitter for the purpose of listening to conversations in the vicinity of the phone'. The phones could be activated as bugs – even when turned off – by remotely installed software. The Department of Justice retrospectively codified this 'roving bug' surveillance amid a prolonged to-and-fro in the courts about the secret services' need to show probable cause.[14]

European bugging

This time, the Europeans were already at it, having set up the legally dubious ENFOPOL system in the late 1990s to allow law enforcement agencies 'real time, full time' access to communications held by internet service providers[15] and to cable TV (Winston Smith couldn't escape by vegeing out in front of the TV). ENFOPOL came into being despite the EU's data-protection drives, which were further destabilized by the internet's borderless operability and by the US preference for letting the industry 'regulate' itself.[16]

The UK codified ENFOPOL with its Regulation of Investigative Powers Act (RIPA) in 2000, which licensed police and intelligence agencies to trawl through people's post, internet, email and telephone records, and criminalized the failure to hand over any encryption keys to investigators – all in the name of fighting crime, pedophilia and terrorism.

Ministerial fiat and function creep were never far away, demolishing the RIPA's balance 'between individual privacy and collective security'. The original nine agencies entitled to use RIPA had grown, by 2008, to 792, including 474 councils, fire brigades and job centers, and RIPA surveillance was extended from terrorists to fouling dogs, under-age smoking and parents who might have given a false home address to get their daughter into an over-subscribed school. By 2007, requests to access phone and email records had risen to over 1,500 per day. Meanwhile, of some 800 complaints made about RIPA abuse to the Investigatory Powers Tribunal, only three were upheld.

The British government exported the principles of RIPA to the EU under its presidency in 2006 as Directive 2006/24/EC, which allowed for the retention of internet, email and telephone data, for investigating and prosecuting 'serious crime, as defined by each Member State in its national law'. The Italians, fighting the mafia, and the Irish, fighting sectarian terrorism, were already doing as much, and they arguably had a case to do so, but now no citizen could expect to retain digital privacy, even when the targeting of specific suspects rather than everyone would have achieved the same objectives.[17] MEPs' efforts to have the data retained for only 12 months and for it to be accessed by warrant only for crimes worthy of a European arrest warrant were stymied.

That the killer information might be stashed on a suspect's home PC and require a warrant and a costly high-profile police raid, which might only tip off a broader criminal network, brooked a new level of international co-operation. Snoops access hard-drives remotely using 'rootkits' or 'remote forensic software', as they legally can in Germany to apprehend terrorists. The European Council Presidency tacitly condoned this for Europe-wide use in 2008 (the only issue being the 'cross-border nature' of the spying), the kind of 'conclusion' or soft legislation that allows pan-EU police and judicial co-operation to cover way more than terrorism, and to stretch well beyond the EU. Soon enough, in 2008, the interior ministers of the G6 (the EU's biggest states) met with the US Homeland Security big guns to discuss accelerating the legalization of these methods of accessing hard-drive.[18]

As surveillance expert David Lyon put it: 'September 11, 2001 was a world event but it was also a globalized event. It had impacts throughout the world because it was a product of globalization. These impacts stimulated further globalizing processes. Among these were increased surveillance flows that presage new patterns of power and social arrangements.'[19] Governments and agencies were already seeking to amass and sift through the nodes and flows of data within their own countries and further beyond – 9/11 simply gave them the excuse and impetus to do so. Such activities often commenced without legal sanction, whereupon public disclosure would not cause their cessation but would goad law-making bodies to legitimize these capers retroactively. Once, such surveillance activity was highly targeted and legally regulated; now it is generally applied, unregulated and absolutely routine.

Whereas investigators once worked surreptitiously to collate data, post 9/11 their work with private firms and internet servers was no longer silent nor secret. Whereas before they would request access, they now issue demands to which corporations say yes without hesitation.

No democratically elected government would countenance being charged with prioritizing the protection of privacy over agencies' capacity to stop mass murder. All the same, the amassing of such vast amounts of data may have created haystacks in which the agencies had to find needles. And the needles were real people that were migrating and traveling across the planet. Immigrants and travelers needed controlling, too, which would take the intrusiveness of surveillance to a new level.

Global migration

Like the TIA and TIPS, 9/11 allowed the US to establish more brash surveillance directly aimed at controlling and monitoring the flows of travelers in and out of the US.

One scheme after 9/11 involved No Fly Lists that were to prevent anyone deemed a 'risk' from flying into or out of the US. These No Fly Lists were to be used in conjunction with the Transportation Screening Administration's Computer Assisted Passenger Pre-Screening Program II (CAPPS II), which was designed to complement travel pattern, citizenship and law enforcement agency intelligence with credit records to assess who might blow up a plane.

Public outcry, and the prospect of failure, led to CAPPS II's abandonment. As the boss of the CIA's top IT developer In-Q-Tel pointed out, standardized formulas are unreliable indicators of creditworthiness – and so must also be unreliable indicators of proclivity for terrorism.[20] But the No Fly Lists continued in use, with no evidence of wrong-doing required to be listed by agents who had their own targets to reach. Suspects found out that they were under suspicion at check-in, when they were least able to prove that they were not terrorists. 'False positive' matches abounded. Senator Edward 'Ted' Kennedy was held up often because 'T Kennedy' was once the alias of a suspected terrorist (along with the name of 7,000 innocent American men) – 'Ted' was just his nickname. The singer Cat Stevens was included on a No Fly List because he had converted to Islam decades before, then Senator Ted Stevens' wife Catherine was added – even though no-one called her Cat. Law professor Walter F McCormick was grounded in 2007 for giving a speech denouncing President Bush's violations of the constitution. Nelson Mandela was on the No Fly List until 2008.

In contrast, prospective suicide bomber Umar Farouk Abdulmutallab – the Underwear Bomber – who tried to blow up a transatlantic flight on Christmas Day 2009 was not on the List. He was on the National Counter Terrorism Center's Terrorist Identities Datamart Environment list, but he was not put on the No Fly List, which is run by the FBI.[21] Umar was the needle in the haystack of 550,000 suspects, being added to by 1,600 people per day in 2009 on the kind of 'reasonable suspicion' that somehow overlooked him.[22]

What the Underwear Bomber did do was accelerate the take-up of No Fly Lists in the UK and apply a technological fix to US inter-agency dysfunctionalism. It was now not enough for passengers to have to carry their belongings onto planes in see-through bags, or to expect their laptops to be seized. Now they could be screened by full-body scanners that produced body images of them completely naked. Deemed a 'virtual strip search' by the ACLU in 2002, the deployment of these scanners had been delayed for years, but as UN Special Rapporteur and privacy expert Martin Scheinin commented, 'the wind changed' with Underwear, and the Department of Homeland Security is now spending over $200 million on 1,000 devices by the end of 2011.[23] Anti-pornography laws prevented the scanners being used to screen children, and yet while they showed up every dangly bit and breast implant, they did not reveal liquid or PETN-based explosives, or anything carried internally.[24]

Behind these efforts to inconvenience and humiliate innocent people lay longer-term plans to get all travelers' data, from their credit-card details down to their biometrics, and this was highly symbolic of how the world was turning upside down. The taking of fingerprints and photos was once reserved for criminals and others who were to be locked up, but now it was being demanded of the overwhelming majority of innocent people seeking to travel and enter the Land of the Free.

Congress had pushed for an automated entry and exit monitoring system for foreigners since the 1990s. The Patriot Act added biometrics to this and the 2002 Enhanced Border Security and Visa Entry Reform Act allowed the dissemination of the data. Post 9/11, over 3,000 Muslim and Middle Eastern immigrants (Israelis and Saudis excepted), together with Central Asians and Indonesians, were interviewed and fingerprinted by immigration services, with suspect lists replete with duplicated names and data-entry errors. The National Security Entry-Exit Registration System followed, making 'no country' exempt and being enveloped into the US Visitor and Immigrant Status Indicator Technology, or US-VISIT.[25] As part of that, from 2004, visitors had to give up one fingerprint. Then it became all ten. Then digital photographs were taken. At first, only the 19 million annual visitors from non-visa-waiver countries were targeted (Brazil reciprocated the compliment of this selective suspicion by fingerprinting all its US visitors and, boy, were they pissed off). Soon, US-VISIT expanded to include the 13 million visitors from visa-waiver countries, including Japan, Singapore, Australasia and most of the EU – not out of any new egalitarianism in US xenophobia but because visa-waivers' biometric passports were not ready.[26] The International Civil Aviation Organization (under pressure from the US) ruled under ICAO 9303 that from 2006 all new passports had to carry biometric data – digital representations of a number of fingerprints and a digital facial image. This data would be 'securely' held on Radio Frequency Identification (RFID) chips made to one global machine-readable standard.

Behind the scenes, the US had long requested data on all visitors but 9/11 made these demands irresistible. In 2002, Europol and the US authorities agreed to exchange traveler information, including data on 'race, political opinions, or religious or other beliefs, or concerning health and sexual life'. This overlooked the need for individuals to consent to this under Europol regulations, or to demand that Europol correct or delete incorrect data about them. No rules on which agencies could access what data were laid out. Statewatch called the agreement 'poorly drafted, ambiguous and contradictory', and concluded that it exceeded 'Europol's mandate and [was] incompatible with [EU] data protection principles'.[27]

Not until 2004 did the EU and the US make a public, codifying agreement of sorts that gave the US Customs and Border Protection Agency 34 different data sets from ticket reservation databases, including passengers' credit card numbers and email, and data like missed flights, last-minute ticket purchases, special food or seating requests. These were to be kept for 3.5 years and sifted by the Automated Targeting System to 'score' passengers, with high scorers winning an interview or being barred from entry to the US. MEPs took the matter to the European Court of Justice over concerns about data sharing and privacy, and the agreement was annulled in 2006. At that point a new agreement appeared, with the required data fields reduced to 19 (many of the 34 simply being doubled up), the data being kept for 15 years and any US agency able to access it. This agreement was signed despite 'serious doubts' about its compatibility with European fundamental rights – and the new deal was done in such a way that MEPs could not vote it down.[28]

The European project
Through function creep fueled by the intoxicating powers of unaccountable law making, the European Union has grown immeasurably in power, with Brussels passing motions on all matters from banking and energy to justice and home affairs. The EU now has a centralized federal entity with its Common Foreign and Security Policy and full diplomatic and military powers by way of successive treaties from Rome to Lisbon. It welcomes its new member states by subjecting their citizens to ever more powerful processes of scrutiny and outright suspicion.

For a long time, supposedly, the European project was about the free movement of goods, materials and people. The 1985 Schengen Agreement between France, Germany and Benelux involved their giving up their mutual borders and created the Schengen Area, its policing facilitated by the Schengen Information System (SIS). This would share police, security, immigration and customs information and pass on alerts about stolen goods and wanted individuals.[29] People considered a 'security risk' would be barred from entry.

With typical European tardiness, the internal borders did not go until 1990, and SIS was not operational until 1995. Meantime, in 1991, the EURODAC system was agreed to, under which the biometrics were taken of refugees and asylum seekers down to the age of 14. EURODAC was not operational until 2003, by which point the Schengen had 13 member states, plus Iceland and Norway, and SIS was deemed to need an upgrade 'to bring about more security' and enable it 'to cope with changing requirements'.[30] The SIS duly changed from being a reporting system into an investigative tool, with over 125,000 access points (since expanded to over half a million[31]) being accessible by the pan-European police entity, Europol, and other entities such as vehicle-license agencies, Eurojust and national police forces. The EU's 1999 'action plan on crime' allowed police forces to exchange, trawl, analyze and add data.[32] Biometrics and digital-scan photographs gleaned from the EU's new Visa Information System (VIS) database of worldwide applicants for EU visas would be added. This time, the biometrics of the EU's own citizens would be included, being mandated for inclusion in all travel documents, passports and ID cards from 2005 onwards, 'enhancing' the VIS data exchange.

Welcome to Europe, where fighting terrorists, criminals and managing immigrants are part and parcel of the same databases and systems; these are becoming almost interchangeable concepts. The EU's Hague Programme proposed to codify this activity, plumping for a 'right balance between privacy and security' that fell firmly on the side of security, declaring that 'information for law enforcement purposes needed by member states should be available to all others'.[33]

The Hague Programme was to be implemented in EU time – so, in 2005, Germany, Austria, Spain, France and the Benelux three signed the Treaty of Prüm, which also built on Schengen and allowed signatories' law enforcement agencies to access fingerprint and DNA databases, and 'special categories of data' – racial or ethnic origin, political opinions, religious beliefs, sexual orientation or health. Also, armed and uniformed police officers from one member state could, in an emergency, enter another state without prior consent, and take any provisional measure to avert 'an imminent danger'.[34]

Prüm was not an official EU treaty per se, but it so neatly resembled the Hague Programme's goals that the EU's German presidency proposed that it should become EU policy, without consultation of Europe's citizens. The European Council's own data-protection expert, Peter Hustinx, lambasted it for 'not sufficiently' considering the 'huge amount' of legal and ethical concerns regarding data protection that Prüm raised. Prüm was, however, rubber-stamped into law, with member states' governments compelled to rewrite their own laws within three years.[35]

As the Prüm row rolled on, in June 2006 the G8's justice and interior ministers met in Moscow to discuss... what? asked Statewatch. A secret thing, the British Home Office replied, something that is 'exempt' from the provisions of the Freedom of Information Act.

More international agreements that peg down the data-sharing net are initiatives like the 2009 Five Country (Canada, Australia, New Zealand, US and UK) Conference on immigration and border security, at which Canada, UK and Australia agreed to share the fingerprint information of asylum seekers, those facing deportation and criminals. The Smart Border Plan, meanwhile, allows the US Department of Homeland Security any information it wants about Canadians and Mexicans.[36]

The EU and Russia have likewise been building on 'common spaces', allowing greater co-operation between FRONTEX and Russia's Federal Border Security Service. FRONTEX utilizes scores of aircraft, helicopters, boats and Unmanned Aerial Vehicles to patrol the EU's home waters and those of affected third countries.[37] It has been criticized by the UNHCR, the European Council on Refugees and the British Refugee Council for employing indiscriminate deterrence that stops both illegal immigrants and anyone seeking sanction under the 1951 Refugee Convention. These are all facets of a new world of remote, electronic government, or e-government.

The death of privacy

Global e-government

For all the anxious knavery of these lawless global efforts to monitor migrants, telecoms and financial transactions, the greatest depths of intrusive, sinister surveillance of individuals are being plumbed in the name of pursuits that are ostensibly very mundane.

Governments worldwide have latched onto IT to make governance more efficient. But it was at the G7 meeting in 1994 that the principle of the 'worldwide information society' was agreed, and the UK and Canada were deputed to explore the best practices of what would be called electronic government, or e-government.

The computerization of government functions and data naturally leads to more 'live' information being to hand, allowing for better co-ordination of services and better application of the resources needed to deliver them. Even better is that all this IT allows for more 'open government' as public servants and politicians are laid more open to contact with citizens through email and blogs. Ordinary individuals and businesses will experience e-government through accessing tax returns online, or even looking at medical records. But there is more to e-government than that. The process towards e-government is a truly global enterprise. The United Nations' e-Government Readiness Index at www.unpan.org lists the progress of all 192 states towards e-government and happily states that e-government will 'transform' state operations and institutions – but does not detail when the world's citizens were consulted about this.

The UK program 'Transformational Government' is a case in point, its brochure referring to citizens as customers as if it were some mega supermarket.[38] And the underlying principles of running either are actually the same. Data hitherto held in distinct departmental 'silos' – like Revenue and Customs or the Driver Vehicle Licensing Agency – would be pooled and shared across departments and agencies, creating a digital montage of individuals further colored by information gleaned from other sources, private and personal. This would enable government to 'tailor' services not just upon individual demand, but as the individual's needs might be assessed 'on the basis of previous information'. These montages would become what Lord Carson in 2002 called 'a single source of truth about us all'. Sir David Varney's 2006 report to the UK Treasury said data would be used to 'develop a deep truth about the citizen, based on their behavior, experiences, beliefs, needs and rights' (similarly to Poindexter's TIA). This 'predict and provide' mindset by definition blocks the ears of government to the demands of its citizens, but for the state to talk of its insights into its citizens in such spiritual terms is an alarming transformation indeed.

By 2020, Varney predicted that 'customer groups [citizens] can choose packages of public service requirements tailored to their needs. Public and private and third-sector partners collaborate across the delivery chain in a way that is invisible to the public. The partners pool their intelligence about the needs and preference of local people, and this informs the design of public services and the tailoring of packages for individuals and groups... across all tiers of central and local government, and other public bodies. The public do not see this process.'[39]

That is not 'open' government. It actually involves individuals' data being open to all, with the UK government unable to confirm that its citizens' data would not be transported overseas. Governments will gain as much insight and power as TIA would have provided, but apparently exercised with greater beneficence.

The Database State report found that a quarter of 46 UK government databases that it reviewed were 'almost certainly' illegal under human rights and data protection laws, over half had significant problems with privacy and fewer than 15 per cent had any substantial basis for protecting privacy.[40] No accurate figure for the actual breakdown costs of 'Transformational Government' are available, yet only about 30 per cent of government IT projects succeed, with dangerous precedents for security as well.

But these considerations are dismissed as Luddite. Central to serving the cause of this global revolution in government is 'identity management', with identities managed by ID cards marking the audit trails of our everyday activities.

1 ACLU 2002, http://nin.tl/9UiRKG 2 *The Surveillance-Industrial Complex*, ACLU 2004, http://nin.tl/dbXSKA 3 Fritz Kramer, *Sincerely Yours*, PBS TV, 2007. http://nin.tl/dCjoEJ 4 *Washington Post*, 23 June 2006, http://nin.tl/9r1VsI 5 Privacy International, 24 Nov 2006, http://nin.tl/bHpAKA 6 http://nin.tl/9xTBjU 7 'EU bank data move ignored legal advice', *New York Times* 29 Jul 2009. 8 ACLU 2004, op cit. 9 Electronic Frontier Foundation, www.eff.org/issues/calea 10 www.fas.org/irp/eprint/psp.pdf 11 *New York Times*, 14 Oct 2007, http://nin.tl/avA345 12 *Washington Post*, 5 Aug 2007, http://nin.tl/9UmRb6 13 www.wired.com 15 Jan 2009, http://nin.tl/bwhMzX 14 Electronic Frontier Foundation www.eff.org/issues/cell-tracking 15 Simon Davies, 'Private Matters', *Index on Censorship* 3/00. 16 David Banisar, 'Big Browser is Watching You', *Index on Censorship* 3/00. 17 ZDNet.co.uk, 6 Apr 2009, http://nin.tl/bLm7ZC 18 Tony Bunyan, *The Shape of Things to Come*, Statewatch.org 19 David Lyon, *Surveillance After 9/11*, Polity Press, 2003. 20 www.wired.com/techbiz/media/news/2003/03/58191 21 www.nctc.gov/docs/Tide_Fact_Sheet.pdf 22 *Washington Post*, 31 Oct 2009, http://nin.tl/9hA2up 23 Martin Scheinin, www.guardian.co.uk 20 Jan 2010, http://nin.tl/cSK9nz 24 http://news.bbc.co.uk/1/hi/uk/8439285.stm 25 Privacy International http://nin.tl/dvHvMz 26 BBC news, 3 Apr 2004, http://nin.tl/ddkhd4 27 Statewatch, 2002, http://nin.tl/cfF7k1 28 Ibid. 29 Richard L Clutterbuck, *Terrorism, drugs, and crime in Europe after 1992*, Routledge, 1990. 30 Schengen: from SIS to SIS II http://nin.tl/aKS2Te 31 EU SIS Access document, 2009, http://nin.tl/aH57wy 32 Statewatch, May 2005, http://nin.tl/a1jgQ2 33 The Hague Programme, http://nin.tl/9Dibib and http://nin.tl/aPibg9 34 EU Justice & Home affairs committee, 7 Jun 2007, http://nin.tl/9QUn2I 35 Digital Civil Rights Network, 20 Jun 2007 http://nin.tl/bJ7C6A 36 censusalerg.org.uk/Canada 37 See footnote 18. 38 UK Cabinet Office, Nov 2005, http://nin.tl/bpFhMQ 39 Convention on Modern Liberty, Feb 2009, http://blip.tv/file/1883559 40 *Database State*, Joseph Rowntree Reform Trust, 2009.

4 The dangers of ID cards

Identity cards have been the pet project of security-minded governments for years. Public anxiety about their implications – and their expense – has derailed their introduction in some Western countries. But that has not stopped the West from pushing the cards on to developing countries, which are now serving as guinea pigs for a globalized ID future.

SUPERMARKETS HAVE BECOME paragons of efficiency. The level of accuracy of data on people shopping in supermarkets is such that local councils in Britain have turned to the nation's largest retail chain, Tesco, for help in compiling population figures, as government numbers are considered 'unreliable', and 'inadequate'.[1]

And as supermarkets have successfully used cards to engender loyalty, so governments use them to enforce obedience. The Conservative Party (in government from 2010) has proposed the notion of 'health miles cards' to tackle the UK's obesity crisis, with people 'gaining points' by losing weight or giving up smoking and entitling themselves to gym memberships, fresh vegetables or priority access for other services. Those continuing to live unhealthy lifestyles would lose some benefits or access to things – the NHS in some areas already requires the obese to lose weight prior to any treatment.[2]

But ID cards are capable of much more than that. RFID-enabled biometric ID cards, also known as e-ID, are in use worldwide. National identity cards have been hawked around the world for years as a 'quack cure seeking an ailment'.[3]

Australia and identity
The ID bandwagon has been weaving all over Australia's roads since 1985, when the government wheeled out the patriotically titled Australia Card

and unique ID number, all checkable against a central register. Conceived to create auditable trails for tax purposes, opening bank accounts or buying real estate, by the time the card had paraded through government departments, 13 agencies had thrown social security fraud, illegal immigration, crime and underage drinking aboard. The card was then hawked to the public for Medicare provision (no card would mean people put their lives in danger) and Medicare entitlement (because foreigners were thieving Medicare). Photos were added and the final Australia Card Bill left plenty of scope for uses not requiring parliamentary approval, while 'voluntary' translated into fines of tens of thousands of dollars for losing the card or not using it as mandated. Concerns over the card's operability, privacy and function creep saw parliament shoot down the card in 1986 and 1987, with public opinion against the card hitting 90 per cent, and triggered the Double Dissolution election of 1987, whereupon it was shelved. It was resurrected in 2005 under the National Identity Security Strategy to combat ID theft and benefit fraud, but was ditched on 26 April 2006 in favour of an Access Card, replacing 17 health and social services cards with a tip-top microchip holding the usual gen and details of children, dependants and diseases; this was to be compulsory from 2010. Parliament put a stake though its heart over privacy concerns, but back from the dead it came in 2007 before Prime Minister Kevin Rudd sealed its tomb with garlic.

ID in the US

National ID cards were terrorized onto the US political agenda by the 9/11 Commission, which cited them as a weapon in the anti-terrorism arsenal. This was writ nationwide under the 2005 REAL ID Act by converting state-issued driving licenses to a single, Federal, machine-readable standard with biometrics, 'to protect against terrorist entry into and activities within the United States'.[4] But of all the things that 9/11 purportedly changed, resistance to an ID card was not one of them, such cards having been suggested and rejected since US citizens were given unique Social Security Numbers in 1936, while President Clinton's 1993 Health Security Card died with his Health Care reforms.

Hence, the REAL ID Act was not before Congress until four years post-9/11, and even then the Act was nailed onto the evocatively titled Emergency Supplemental Appropriations Act for Defense, the Global War on Terror and Tsunami Relief 2005 and was given little time for debate. Homeland Security Secretary Michael Chertoff denied it was a national ID card while envisaging it would be used to 'cash a check, hire a baby-sitter, board a plane' by May 2008. By then, the only progress was 19 states having passed motions against REAL ID. The DHS estimated that just federalizing the Department of Motor Vehicles to obtain a driver's license would cost $23.1 billion over 10 years, then applied some dodgy accounting and came up with a revised $9.9 billion figure in 2008. Still they seek to press ahead, with a 2017 deadline.

Americans were told that ID cards would stop dirty illegal workers taking low-paid farm jobs and get them deported. But as illegal workers already lack the right papers, they're not going to bother with an ID card. As the ACLU said of the US's pending biometric ID-based Employment Eligibility Verification System, only legitimate companies would enroll and take on its bureaucratic hassles, its costly biometric readers and its IP connections to cater for the US's 150 million workers. This would further advantage black-market employers exploiting the estimated 12 million undocumented immigrant workers who would still work below the radar.[5] 'Crooked insiders' would always exist and sell authenticating documents (in the late

The dangers of ID cards

19th century, Chinese immigrants to the US established a vast trans-Pacific enterprise in fake identity documents, fabricating familial links and histories to counter increasingly draconian and overtly racist US immigration policies).

Blair's baby

The UK's ID card scheme was a near-decade long case study in duplicity and function creep. It was first peddled by the Blair government, even after 9/11, as an entitlement card to access social security and fight fraud – although the US and Australia have suffered worse fraud since a supposedly secure, single point of reference became the accepted norm. Ambivalent public support for such a card mattered less than that the G8 justice and interior ministers had been pushing for biometric ID cards and the transnational sharing of data since 2004.[6] That inspired the UK in 2005, in its presidency of the European Union, to lay down the standards for a Europe-wide, biometric-equipped ID card. In 2006, the EU was thereby partly blamed for 'forcing' the British to batter ID cards into law – public unease was growing. At one point the UK government claimed that the massive amounts of data it was asking for – over 50 categories of personal information, plus a head shot, all 10 fingerprints and any other requested biometric – were required under the European Schengen Treaty – although Schengen did not require such data, and the UK was not a signatory to it anyway.

All this information was to be retained on the National Identity Register, a central 'meta-database' to be cross-referenced with hundreds of other databases, private and public, every time someone applied for a mortgage, bought cigarettes or picked up a parcel from the post office. The technology to be used was untried; the system's scope for failure unquantifiable.

The cards were then repitched as the means to

'tackle terrorism, crime and illegal immigration'. ID cards and passports identified the bombers involved in 9/11, 7/7 and the 2004 Madrid bombings – but only after the events. Former MI5 chief Dame Stella Rimington said the intelligence services viewed ID cards as 'absolutely useless' if they could be forged.

Public support began to tank. The European Association for e-identity and Security (members included London's Metropolitan police, the European Commission and arms-makers and security sellers Thales and Siemens) helpfully advised the UK government to flag up the card's 'commercial and business value'.[7]

To no avail. Within days of taking office in May 2010, the UK's Coalition government binned the cards. The saga may not be over yet. But the UK's lack of an ID card puts it in a small minority within the 27 states of the European Union and the three additional Schengen members. The Council of the European Union continues to chart the harmonization of ID cards and passports and seeks to collect more data and add more biometrics to them. The Council may 'consult' the European Parliament about this process, but it is not obliged to do so under the Lisbon Treaty.

ID cards in the Global South

Whereas Belgium uses modern encryption methods and local storage to protect privacy and prevent data-sharing, French ID cards do not create an audit trail to an ID database and Germany has no centralized database of all its information, the UK card would have enabled anyone in authority – public or private – to question individuals who stand out for reasons of personal appearance, demeanor or racial profiling. This has been a problem in other countries with ID cards, such as Malaysia, which introduced the world's first microchip-installed, biometric cards, MyKad ('my', as in property of the state) in September 2001, updating the ID card systems left in place by the departing British colonial authorities. The card, compulsory at age 18, contains biometrics, personal data including religion (for Muslims), and passport information (although it's not a passport), and health data and serves as ID, driver's license, e-cash, and as a distrusted ATM card. Even before its introduction it was planned for use in cyber cafés or in elections (prompting fears of an electoral chilling effect on anyone voting against the government, particularly government employees), while Malay consumer associations attacked the lack of guidelines as to who could access MyKad or why. Slowly the card changed from being an optional entity to a de facto requirement for numerous government and private services like security guards demanding people surrender their cards before entering a building.[8] Kuala Lumpur's Islamic religious authorities sought portable card readers to 'instantly verify' whether Muslim couples found in 'close proximity' – standing having a chat – were married,[9] while police and religious authorities use ID cards to harass particular groups, such as transsexuals.[10]

In 2009 India announced 'the biggest Big Brother project ever conceived'. This would involve issuing biometric ID cards to its 1.2 billion people, with this one card replacing the dozens of ID certificates issued by India's numerous states. With only seven per cent of the population registered to pay income tax, and the Electoral Commission's voter lists being mostly corrupted by political manipulation, it was unclear what the primary sources of information would be, let alone how some 60 government departments would cease their bureaucratic turf wars and unite behind the scheme. The proposed ID-card scheme would require a vast electronic infrastructure for which India has no precedent, would be built by an Indian electronics manufacturing base that doesn't yet exist, and be, as advisors Ernst & Young said, 'impregnable', something hitherto unknown in IT.[11]

The ID-card schemes adopted or proposed by governments in the rich world have often been test-driven in the developing world. Belgium's colonial legacy to Rwanda included ID cards demarcating the Tutsis from the Hutus, a divide-and-rule distinction that enabled the Hutus' 'incredibly efficient' murder of a million Tutsis in 100 days in 1994. Scores of thousands of Rwandan refugees escaped to the Democratic Republic of Congo (DRC), where, in 2002, they must have been alarmed by the UNHCR's man in Kinshasa saying the 440,000 refugees in the country were in need of ID documents, 'particularly for security reasons. Not having an ID card means that a refugee can run into all kinds of problems and get questioned by the authorities',[12] leaving one to wonder whether the problem lies with the poorest of the poor, or with the oppressive authorities.

The dangers of ID cards

Another line spun to governments in the Global South is that ID cards are integral to establishing databases that are 'a basic necessity in a democracy', as the World Bank assistance program in Côte d'Ivoire pitched it,[13] and which are needed to underpin credible elections – though every Western democracy has had elections without cards since voting began. In 2009, the DRC duly issued 11.8 million voter ID cards for its own national elections.

But ID cards are as good at killing democracy. In 2002, Robert Mugabe's Zimbabwean government made it illegal for people to move about without ID cards, on pain of fines or jail, in the name of combating crime and terrorism, despite the Supreme Court deeming them unconstitutional. In reality the cards were but one measure to wreck the following year's presidential elections, which Mugabe 'won' just prior to setting Zimbabwe staggering onto the path of murderous insularity. ID cards were all about security – specifically that of Mugabe's regime.[14]

Gambians, meanwhile, were bidden to replace their existing ID cards with biometric cards in August 2009 as part of making a modern society, but observers noted that Gambia, decades post-independence, had yet to agree a unanimously accepted standard as to who qualified for citizenship, their rights and, more importantly, what the 'excluded' were to do.[15] Biometrics would not solve the problems of a bureaucracy unable to record births and deaths, or issue citizen numbers at birth, or that had bogged down the issuing of paper cards for years.[16]

South Africa demonstrates the canyon between what the state expects of its citizens and what it delivers itself. In 2005, bureaucrats admitted that replacing the existing paper-based cards with biometric-chip cards would cost 120 rand each in a country where the minimum wage was 4.10 rand per hour. The card would also take five years to go nationwide, in a land where people have to wait four years for new birth certificates or queue for 12 hours to get updated driving licenses. [17] The state's requirement for citizens to have ID just to function on a daily basis does not mean that the state reciprocates by functioning properly. In 2009, one 22-year-old man, sole guardian and provider for his four siblings, committed suicide for want of an ID that would allow him to work. A local official had refused to issue a card, destroyed his attestations and accused him of being a foreigner. A Department of Home Affairs hotline for people to complain about civil service ineptitude, incompetence and arrogance failed to work. [18]

Fancy biometrics do not help willfully dysfunctional bureaucracies. Institutionalized sclerosis, excessive costs and incompetence bedevil Uganda's government and frustrate citizens from obtaining voter cards, new birth certificates, driving licenses and resident permits. National ID cards were pushed as the cure-all solution, before being dropped in 2003 as the card procurement process was allegedly tainted with malpractice, bribery and corruption. [19] ID cards were then reintroduced piecemeal for things like the 2012 census, but Uganda's foreign ministry said in October 2009 this process might be urgently expedited – notwithstanding problems of implementation – to counter the threat of attacks by Somalia-based, al-Qaeda-linked militants upon Kampala. How any card would stop direct attacks, no-one explained, but the foreign minister felt it necessary to stress that Somali refugees in Uganda were not going to be interned. [20] The sad fact that oil and trouble always go together may provide some explanation for the cards – Western oil companies are enhancing demands for security as Uganda comes onstream as a major African oil exporter.

Uganda is also having ID cards pushed upon it as part of its membership of the East African

The dangers of ID cards

Community (EAC), along with Kenya, Tanzania, Rwanda and Burundi. The EAC is working towards the free movement of capital and citizens and possible monetary union by 2012, following the model of the European Union. Indeed, the European Union Central Bank is overseeing the EAC's creation and its developing capital markets, planning, intra-EAC affairs,

Green surveillance

Green legislation and environmental monitoring are playing their part in the advance of the surveillance society.[1] Our carbon footprints are unique eco-equivalents of our fingerprints, our patterns of consumption leaving quantifiable data from which we can be identified, and much can be inferred about our lives and attitudes to the world. 'Green' measures are excellent ways of inducing people to accept micro-management of their lives, as governments harvest our spending and transaction data to help us reduce our consumption and carbon emissions.[2] One EU scheme to encourage recycling has microchips in rubbish bins that denote their owner and allow them to be warned or fined if the bin is too heavy, suggesting that they are failing to recycle sufficiently. Reaching the British government's Carbon Emissions Reduction Target through the Heatseekers plan involves environmental officers assessing the energy efficiency of homes, and advising homeowners about insulation, by taking thermal images of their houses – without their knowledge or consent.[3]

One notable 'green' measure in the US was the 'cash for clunkers' campaign in 2009, in which the government paid drivers to trade in their gas-guzzlers for leaner models. However, car dealers logging onto the scheme's website were informed that their computer was 'considered a Federal computer system and is the property of the United States Government... all files on this system may be intercepted, monitored, recorded, copied, audited, inspected and disclosed to any number of officials and agencies, domestic and foreign,' with consent implicit.[4]

Environmental and anti-terror measures often go hand in hand. Britain's controversial Regulation of Investigative Powers Act 2000 was brought in to fight terrorism, but is better known for its use catching fly-tippers (those who dump garbage illegally). London's Ealing Council is also fighting fly-tipping and enviro-crimes by installing mini-CCTV cameras hidden in bricks and fake baked bean tins and linked to a council CCTV control center – there is the function-creep bonus of nailing people who simply put their garbage out on the wrong day.[5]

Congestion Charge Zones in cities across Europe require drivers to pay to enter them on weekdays, a system enforced by CCTV that and trade, backed by bureaus of statistics, banking and ID cards.[21] One non-negotiable component of the EAC is a harmonized system of ID cards doubling as passports, which was 'agreed' to despite Tanzania's resistance on the grounds that it does not have ID cards at present.

There is nothing democratic about having cards

---

notes their registration plates. However, London police have exclusive dispensation from the Data Protection Act to access the Zone's CCTV 24/7 to combat 'the enduring vehicle-borne terrorist threat to London'.[6] This system also links into the UK's nationwide Advanced Number Plate Recognition CCTV system, which can track 50 million number plates every day, built in the name of better traffic management but open for all levels of police to 'fully and strategically exploit', a move that Privacy International said 'would never be allowed in any other democratic country'. Similarly, the EU is pushing for every car to have GPS installed, linked to its Galileo satellite system, making for a continent-sized pay-per-kilometer system, while Galileo is also being built to monitor the environment and for use in future military contexts.

In another way, environmentalism is now almost equated with terrorism. At the 2009 Copenhagen climate talks, Danish police pre-emptively detained a staggering 900 demonstrators under a controversial law passed just weeks before the summit.[7] No arrest, no charge, no consent to being detained, but personal details taken and ultimately uploaded onto a larger surveillance list run by Europol that defines environmental protesters as 'radicals' along with Islamists, nationalists, global justice campaigners et al – as did the FBI under Hoover's regime. Among the details logged: information about demonstrators' friends, family, neighbors, internet usage, political beliefs and psychological traits. The Europol list is of people who have not necessarily committed a serious crime or raised their voice in pursuit of an ideology or cause – they just have the potential to do so.[8] In some cases criminal acts have been incited by *agents provocateurs* planted in campaigning groups by the groups they oppose – as when business counter-intelligence group C2i infiltrated groups like Plane Stupid so as to incite them to self-destruction.[9]

1 Adam Curtis, *The Power Of Nightmares*, BBC TV 2006. 2 Privacy International http://nin.tl/culB4a. 3 *Daily Mail*, 22 Jan 2009 http://nin.tl/aogUoi 4 *The Times* 7 Aug 2009. http://nin.tl/99iUNm 5 *Daily Telegraph* 21 Mar 2007. 6 Henry Porter, *Suspect Nation*, Channel 4, 2006. 7 *The Guardian* 26 Nov 2009 http://nin.tl/97lPZQ 8 www.guardian.co.uk, 8 June 2010 http://nin.tl/cVFtbh 9 timesonline http://nin.tl/9zSKQG

foisted upon people, but Western 'aid' and bank loans are sometimes tied to the introduction of ID schemes. IMF assistance to Burundi was conditional on the country introducing ID cards, to 'improve transparency and public finance management'. All government employees from ministers to teachers were to get their own central file and ID number – perhaps so that IMF HQ could watch a Burundi teacher buy classroom chalk in real-time.[22] Teachers were first to get ID cards under a three-year IMF deal with Sierra Leone in 2001.[23] Similar IMF diktats were imposed on Uganda, where biometric cards were to be distributed to bank customers across the financial sector. The government had to explain to the IMF in June 2008 that introducing national ID would take 'somewhat longer' than envisaged, in no small part due to the scheme's high cost. Tanzania's absence of ID cards could not last – a bank established in the country in mid-2009 aimed to empower poorer women, who would only need $2 to open an account – so long as they had an ID card.[24] The benefits to Tanzanians and Ugandans of these IMF-mandated ID systems is altogether less clear than the benefit to the private companies that provide them, such as US firm LaserCard, which started delivering biometric cards to oil-exporting Angola as part of the country's 'modernization'.[25]

Other regional set-ups that plan to be absorbed into the One World of ID are the Andean Community of Nations, the Union of South American Nations (their entry presaged by the introduction of biometric ID cards into Mexico) and the Co-operation Council for the Arab States of the Gulf. These will help create the tectonic plates of international identity management in an e-governed world.

Surveillance and immigration controls
One reason why governments in the Global North are so keen on tying loans and debt relief to ID schemes is

that these will enable them to control future waves of migration. The EU thinks it has a problem with illegal immigration and seeks the co-operation of third states to curb this 'at its roots'. Since 2007, the EU agency FRONTEX has advised on the uptake of cards, while also sweeping the borders clear of immigrants. It is eco-refugees who will contribute most to the migrant tsunami that the North really fears. In early 1990, UK Prime Minister Margaret Thatcher warned that climate change would lead to 'a great migration of population away from the areas of the world liable to flooding, and from areas of declining rainfall and therefore of spreading desert. Those people will be crying out not for oil wells but for water.'[26] Rather than controlling their own emissions that fuel climate change, the rich states of the Global North prefer to build migration and security defenses to dam at source the rising tide of humanity that will come washing at their shores, despite pleas from the likes of Bangladesh's finance minister for 'our development partners to honor the natural right of persons to migrate' from a land of 165 million souls where 60 per cent of the land is less than five meters above sea level.[27]

The UN estimates that, since 1990, some 10 million people have migrated across the porous borders between rich world and poor, forced to move by environmental degradation, weather-related disasters and desertification. The UN estimates that this figure will rise 15-fold over the coming half century, and of the 28 countries it lists as at 'extreme risk' from climate change, 22 are in Africa. Maybe if the money spent on ID cards were spent on development, the locals might become happy enough not to want to leave.

1 'Every Little Helps on Migrants', *Metro*, 7 Mar 2008. 2 *London Lite*, 4 Sep 2007. 3 Peter Lilley, www.guardian.co.uk 30 Jun 2002, http://nin.tl/9oUaaB 4 Privacy International, http://nin.tl/bjxCEm 5 ACLU anti card testimony. 6 Privacy International, http://nin.tl/bDVAhD 7 Statewatch.org http://nin.tl/9EIg30 8 'Malaysia to fingerprint all new-born children', *The Register*,

The dangers of ID cards

4 May 2005. **9** Privacy International http://nin.tl/aBMc82 **10** Sarah Stewart, 'Twilight life of Malaysia's Muslim transsexuals', AFP, 6 Sep 2009. **11** *The Times*, 15 July 2009, http://nin.tl/am4P6F **12** UNHCR, 22 Nov 2002, www.unhcr.org/3dde42814.html **13** World Bank, http://nin.tl/bEXNuV **14** BBC news, 22 Nov 2001, http://nin.tl/dnGl3C **15** *The Observer*, 18 Aug 2009, http://nin.tl/9fpRlY **16** Allafrica.com 17 Aug 2009, http://nin.tl/9zs7EQ **17** *The Register*, 26 Oct 2005, http://nin.tl/b5WNuc **18** BBC news, 31 Aug 2009, http://nin.tl/ataYpr **19** Allafrica.com 12 Oct 2009, http://nin.tl/bHvWqe **20** *Daily Monitor*, Uganda, www.monitor.co.ug **21** See footnote 59. **22** IMF 2006, http://nin.tl/98NKtr **23** IMF 2004, http://nin.tl/9pX4ll **24** BBC news, 28 Jul 2009, http://nin.tl/aQDSMp **25** http://nin.tl/96HPY9 **26** Dinyar Godrej, *No-Nonsense Guide to Climate Change*, New Internationalist, 2006. **27** John Vidal, www.guardian.co.uk, 4 Dec 2009, http://nin.tl/bv8rPb

5 The technology of control

The technology once employed only by movie spies is increasingly becoming part of everyday life, from the ubiquitous surveillance camera through microchip trackers and biometric scanners to harnessing DNA.

SURVEILLANCE DEPENDS ON technology – databases are filled with data of great variety and amassed in different ways. Possibly the most overt and undiscriminating (so far) form of surveillance is the Closed Circuit Television camera – aka CCTV – found in bus, train, plane, public space, washroom and cellphone, the world over.

CCTV first saw the light of day in 1942, when Siemens AG installed cameras at Peenemunde, Germany, to observe test launches of the V2 rockets being developed to bomb London and Rotterdam.[1] Initial civilian applications for CCTV were for monitoring traffic, while consumers came to be targeted by department stores from the late 1960s, with cameras becoming integral to the design and management of the vast shopping malls that erupted worldwide from the late 1970s and 1980s atop the credit-card consumer boom.

The value of the global CCTV market hit $13 billion by the end of 2009 and is expected to grow at an annual rate of 21 per cent between 2010 and 2012. Asia will account for 45 per cent of the market, with regional growth led by China.[2] CCTV was first used in Beijing to monitor traffic but proved invaluable in arresting protestors during and after the 1989 Tiananmen Square massacre. Today, the city of Shenzhen exemplifies China's vast appetite for CCTV, with over two million CCTV cameras planned for installation by 2011, all connected to a single nationwide network. US firms such as Honeywell, General Electric, United Technologies and IBM are cashing in on the Chinese boom, where the internal CCTV market was worth $4.1 billion in 2007 alone, while Chinese firms like Aebell Electrical Technology are NASDAQ-listed and sell into the $200-billion US domestic security market.

It was the UK, home of George Orwell, that for years led the way in CCTV. Its use there exploded after 1993, when shopping mall CCTV in Bootle, England, showed toddler Jamie Bulger being abducted by two 10-year-old boys who later murdered him. Amid a 'national moral panic', 480 councils applied for government grants for open-street CCTV. By 1996, nearly every major British city center had CCTV – Brighton hosted the first anti-CCTV demonstration in 1997.

The UK has since been the world's foremost CCTV nation, with an official total of over four million cameras, public and private, a quarter of the global total. The average Londoner is filmed by 300 cameras every day.[3] These figures are by now, however, gross underestimates, as the size and cost of video cameras has been so vastly reduced that not only are they now routinely included in mobile phones worldwide, but even taxis and corner shops can afford their own CCTV set-up. The giant insect mandibles that used to hang off buildings to place public spaces under surveillance have been replaced by cameras more like snowdrop flowers.

How good CCTV is in its primary capacity, as a tool for fighting crime, has been ambiguous at best. In 1999 the Scottish Centre for Criminology called CCTV's promises of reduced crime and reduced fear of crime, 'over-hyped'. In 2002, the National Association for the Care and Resettlement of Offenders found that crime had fallen in only 13 cities out of 24 where CCTV was installed. US studies showed CCTV had had little to no overall impact on crime rates when compared with other variables, like better lighting for parked cars, more police patrols or broader social-economic themes.[4] CCTV may only displace crime from its immediate vicinity, and villains can wear hoods or just dodge the cameras, as did a 'very street smart' gang one night on London's Isle of Dogs as they dished out six random beatings, all out of CCTV sight.[5] The UK's principal customer and advocate for CCTV, the Home Office, reported in 2005 of 13 different surveillance projects that 'policy makers could be forgiven for concluding that CCTV should not be continued'; the projects, it said, were badly conceived and managed and their virtues 'oversold' by eager industry suppliers.[6] As one detective chief inspector told the Security Document World Conference in 2008, the UK's CCTV systems were an 'utter fiasco', helping to solve just three per cent of London's street robberies. Claims that residents demand CCTV as it makes them feel safer have also been countered, with the 2005 Home Office report showing that the public knew CCTV was only of use as a 'comfort blanket'.[7] However, the report concluded: 'There was no pressure to have it [CCTV] removed, and there were no major concerns... about infringement of civil liberties.'

In 2006 came talking CCTV. The English city of Middlesbrough installed cameras equipped with loudspeakers through which staff in the control center could publicly upbraid litterers, ordering them to pick up the packaging they had just dropped.[8] Then there was listening CCTV, aimed at detecting the 'sounds of aggression or fear', and trialed in British cities following successful use in Dutch cities, detention centers and many schools.[9] One in ten teachers surveyed by the Association of Teachers and Lecturers knew of CCTV cameras in their school's washrooms.

Information about such systems' installation and usage is often scant and public acceptance often flows from public ignorance. There is a disturbing lack of data as to who is watching the watchers in an industry Liberty has called 'dangerously unregulated'. Advisory group Camera Watch found that CCTV installations did not meet the prescribed guidelines in 90 per cent of cases.

One problem is that cameras are only as good as the people watching the mesmerizing monitors: operators' attention has been shown to collapse to unacceptable levels after just 20 minutes.[10] Meanwhile the quality of CCTV installation, recording, filing and maintenance – particularly of analog cameras containing film – varies so widely as often to render the material unusable for identification purposes.[11]

Advanced Facial Recognition

One favored solution is to replace analog imagery with digital and replace humans with computers. Advanced Facial Recognition (AFR) technology that enables computers – in theory – to identify individuals and take surveillance to a whole new level originated in 1993 as part of the US government's war on drugs.[12] The efficacy of AFR is questionable. The introduction of AFR by London's Newham council to track repeat offenders, for instance, proved so useless that the council instead turned its CCTV footage into a subscription TV channel, with residents spotting local offenders whose details were pasted on-screen – itself problematic given that criminals could equally use the system to find victims or to avoid the police.

But AFR compatibility underpins the demand for digital photographs in ID cards, driving licenses and passports. Interpol deems AFR as integral to its $1-billion 'global security initiative' and wants immigration officers to cross-check the world's 800 million international travelers against its database of fugitives and suspects. Britain's first AFR gates duly started working at Manchester airport in 2009.[13] The claim is that just as Google can in milliseconds find that one internet page from the trillion online, so AFR will do the same for people.[14] And Google will help. Google StreetView seeks to have every street in the world viewed online courtesy of its camera-carrying cars, notwithstanding privacy protests in Japan and complaints to the UK's Information Commissioner. Already, Google Earth allows people to view the whole world – down to the car outside your house – from satellites. In 2009, Google planned to link up its StreetView with the CCTV systems of London's Metropolitan Police and Westminster Council.[15] It is clear that many public and private camera systems are no longer 'closed circuit' but are interlinked to one another. Google is officially making that global.

Alongside AFR is Video Content Analysis, with computers programmed in behavior recognition to pick out anyone loitering near an ATM or potential bombers or graffiti artists in the transit systems of London, New York, Rome and Tel Aviv.[16] BAe Systems' Onboard Threat Detection System, being developed for an EU security project, involves fingernail-sized cameras being installed into airliner seats to monitor passengers' every blink and twitch.[17] Microphones would pick up whispered remarks, which would then be computer scanned and matched against the passenger's profile to pre-empt a suicide bomb attack or hijacking. BAe Systems is working on CCTV that automatically tracks 'criminal postures' and 'distinctive characteristics such as the way someone walks or smiles... for use during large-scale public events'.[18]

These days police forces regularly use Unmanned Aerial Vehicles (UAVs), which are employed by the military for reconnaissance and air strikes, as with the US in Afghanistan and Iraq and with Israel in Palestine. A British Army recruitment advert depicted a soldier flying a UAV by remote control from a laptop, as if war were a video game. The use of UAVs against civilians covers border patrols, as with the Russians in the Caucasus, the Americans over Mexico, and EU customs agents and border police over the English Channel, the Mediterranean and the Balkans.[19] British police use UAVs to film events like British National Party rallies or rioting druids at Stonehenge, while BAe Systems and Kent police are preparing for their use in the 2012 Olympics by practicing on bad drivers, protestors and fly-tippers, with the perpetrators identified and their activities beamed live to the world.[20]

Radio Frequency Identification (RFID)

Identification by CCTV can be thwarted by someone wearing a mask. The Radio Frequency Identification chip, or RFID, however, is harder to foil. RFIDs are tiny microchips that contain unique identifying data and can be stuck on or inserted into anything or any person so that they can be identified and located. Some RFIDs actively transmit data, others are passive emitters that need electronic scanning, like barcodes. RFIDs became globally ubiquitous through their effectiveness in tracking freighted goods, then were extended to shifting stock in stores, with their concealment in freight, packages, bags or clothing posing no barrier to their being identified and tracked through time and space.

IBM helped to pioneer RFID, and its US patent application 20020116274 showed what the corporation had in mind: 'The widespread use of RFID tags on merchandise such as clothing would make it possible for the locations of people, animals and objects to be tracked on a global scale – a privacy invasion of Orwellian proportions.'[21] In 2003, Benetton was found out literally trying to get into its customers' pants by inserting 15 million RFIDs in its Sisley women's undergarments range, provoking the 'I'd rather go naked' boycott campaign of Benetton goods. The European Commission's efforts to protect consumers from RFID-enabled *Minority Report*-style marketing saw it urging organizations to carry out their own privacy impact assessments and risk-minimization techniques – effectively leaving it to the vested interests of industry to sort things out.[22] Meanwhile, various US states have passed laws protecting citizens from excessive RFID-enabled intrusions. But these only work for Americans. Everyone else gets the full scan.

It's all about consent, especially when RFIDs are implanted into humans. Indonesia does not require the consent of AIDS carriers to chip them,[23] and inmates in Minnesota's panoptical prisons get no sympathy for being chipped.[24] Implanting Alzheimer's patients in Florida may enable their identification should they wander off, but can they have given informed consent for the invasive act of being chipped?[25] Why wrist-borne MedicAlert bracelets containing the same data would not work is unclear – though even these contain chips that some claim cause tumors,[26] produce electromagnetic interference or fail to function properly.[27] Celebrities, politicians and royalty have chipped themselves as a counter-kidnapping move – although kidnappers could locate them first by their RFID and then remove it, with any level of mutilation, to prevent further tracking.

Whereas most people could not stomach a RFID implant, they carry them out of convenience. RFID-bearing swipe cards are central to the running of mass transit systems from Washington DC and Chicago to London, Delhi and Hong Kong, all installed by Cubic Transportation Systems (part of US defense contractor Cubic Corporation). London's transport chiefs bribed commuters into taking the Oyster card (the equivalent of SmarTrip in Washington DC and MetroCard in New York) by making Oyster trips cheaper and cash-bought paper tickets extortionate. At a swipe the authorities tapped priceless reams of commuter-flow macro-data, while every individual's journey across the networks is tracked (the few anonymous Oysters notwithstanding). At least up until 2008, the Oyster card used the Mifare chip, which Dutch security researchers hacked using a laptop, suggesting not only that the information held on millions of Oyster cards was insecure, but that the thousands of government offices, hospitals and schools worldwide using the same chip for their pass cards were also at risk. This hacking caused the Dutch government to require the immediate replacement of 120,000 civil servant cards.[28]

In shops, however, swiped transactions are speedier and make for fewer errors, cash robberies become obsolete and the handling and shipping costs of cash become redundant.[29] RFIDs also allow for credit cards, travel passes and mobile phones to become all-in-one combinations, like the O_2-Nokia combo.[30] Scientists at Royal Dutch Shell in Canada have tested RFIDs and found cards with nominal ranges of just a few centimeters could be detected up to 65 centimeters away. In a crowded place like a shopping arcade or a packed commuter train, anyone with a pocket scanner could pick up thousands of readings.

If the security of RFIDs can be compromised, then having all the world's passports chipped may seem rash – if not downright stupid if done in the name of security – but that is what the US pushed for post 9/11. Even so, polls showed over 90 per cent of US consumers did not want RFIDs on privacy grounds,[31] and there was sufficient domestic resistance that the State Department rebranded its RFID-enabled passports as 'contactless smart-cards' (some argued that this was less to allay fears about universal tracking, than to satisfy groups like Resistance for Christ, which had likened RFIDs to the Mark of the Anti-Christ – and were also core Republican voters).[32] Nevertheless, the US government pressed ahead with RFID-chipped biometric passports, which it said were being demanded under global standard ISO 14443[33] – despite the 2006 Dutch TV program 'Nieuwslicht', which demonstrated how an RFID-enabled passport and reader could be hijacked by a PC and the encrypted data reconstituted so as to make a clone passport.[34] In 2009, hacker Chris Paget used a $250 device to clone scores of RFID-equipped e-passports and driving licenses of San Franciscans while passing them in his car.[35]

Just like SWIFT for global banking, establishing one global standard means that anyone can enter Fort Knox through the rotted washroom window at the back, and a new security system actually makes people less secure. Governments may do very well out of it, however. The average protestor may wear a mask, turn off their mobile and leave their ID at home, but the RFID in their clothes would still give them away to any network of scanners, static or carried by undercover police. A million protestors on an anti-war march become manageable, as every individual can be identified, tracked down and dealt with one by one, avoiding the bad PR of baton-wielding police. This may explain why China, where corruption and social inequality have sparked riots and protests nationwide, had by 2008 spent over $6 billion providing up to a billion RFID-embedded ID cards, benefitting itself and the likes of the Motorola, Texas Instruments and Infineon corporations.[36]

Biometrics
Much of the data retained on RFIDs – in passports particularly, but also for use in ATMs, starting cars, using vending machines or registering at school – is biometric. Biometrics are the digital measurements of our unique fingerprints, irises, faces and vein patterns that can be used to identify us. But the uniqueness of every individual's biometrics does not mean they

cannot be forged, hacked or hijacked in some way.

Fingerprints were in use in ancient Babylon and by Chinese bureaucrats to authenticate clay tablets and seals on documents. These functions were reprised by British civil servant William Herschel in 19th-century India to combat rampant fraud and for social control. The colonials' 'theater of power' involved natives working to task within strictly codified, uniform and uniformed roles. Like the police in urbanizing western Europe, the rulers needed to identify 'criminal tribes and castes' – criminality being an ethnic trait – and others the state 'sought to control or eliminate'. Fingerprinting thereby came into widespread use as a means of mass identification and classification by caste.[37]

By the late 19th century, photography was also proving to be a cheap and easy way of identifying prisoners, although ageing, facial hair, or nuances like skin tone and bad lighting could distort an image, while there was no means then of transmitting photographs. As a result, France's Alphonse Bertillon devised a range of 11 categories of exacting, numerically digitized bodily measurements measuring facial features, hands and feet that could be readily sent by Morse code worldwide, allowing subjects to be tracked 'across time and space in ways photography alone could not'.[38] However, the veracity of the Bertillonage system was undermined by the simple human frailties of inexperience and expediency that meant the regimen of taking and storing exacting measurements was not always rigorously applied. Variation and error crept in. Felons escaped and the wrong people got busted.

Systems like Bertillonage were adapted and refined into anthropological studies and eugenics theories, with the Nazis keen to see if there were common physical traits to be identified among the 'criminal' races of Jews and Romanies. These days, fingerprints and DNA are still used to identify criminals, and researchers are working on DNA coding that indicates a predisposition to criminality.

But human error still makes for flaws. Hence the FBI's 17-day detention of Oregon lawyer Brandon Mayfield, after they linked him to the Madrid bombings of 11 March 2004 through partial prints taken from detonators related to the blasts. Spanish police insisted the FBI double-check the prints, meanwhile matching them to an Algerian suspect. Mayfield was subsequently cleared of all charges and the FBI apologized, but he had a narrow escape.[39] Still, such cases are deemed rare and it is widely accepted that the cost of keeping the world safe might have to include some innocents going down.

Industry and commerce have seized upon fingerprints as but one biometric in a 'secure' age of identity-based lives, with their use standardized for consumers using cellphones or computers, starting cars or activating door locks.[40] However, the mandated taking of biometrics for passports and ID cards raises concerns over consent. Many take great offense at being fingerprinted like criminals – little realizing that we are all suspects in the world of risk management.

In 2005, someone convinced the Malay police that they needed the fingerprints of children even younger than 12 years old for their MyKid card (the children's version of MyKad). Aware that software existed that could chart the changes in fingerprints wrought by natural growth over the years, it was decided to fingerprint all new-born babies.[41] Similarly, in 2007, the British government pondered fingerprinting 11-15 year-olds for a new ID card. Unfortunately, this was less controversial than it might appear as tens of thousands of schools worldwide were already demanding children hand over their fingerprints for cards to take out library books, for registration, and use in the canteen – why library cards or ticking a

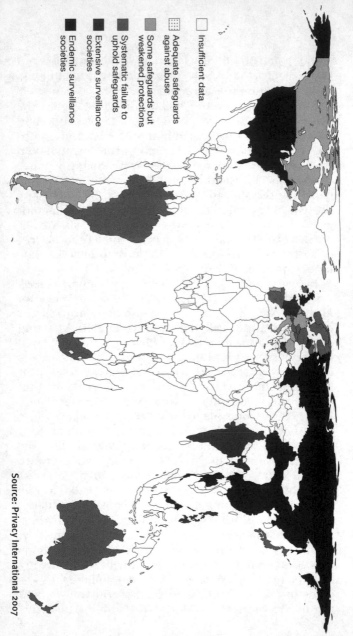

Levels of surveillance by country

Insufficient data

Adequate safeguards against abuse

Some safeguards but weakened protections

Systematic failure to uphold safeguards

Extensive surveillance societies

Endemic surveillance societies

Source: Privacy International 2007

child's name off at registration no longer suffice is not clear. Biometric cards in schools do not stop bullying, stabbings and shootings. What they do make possible is for children's reading habits to be monitored individually, and for children to be sifted according to ethnicity and gender by any group – councils, social services or the police – seeking to pre-empt potential problems by way of statistical probabilities.

Meanwhile parents are often the last to know their children are being fingerprinted, or else are offered a deal they can't refuse. Morley High School in Leeds decreed that any child opting out of fingerprinting could not have school meals, a likely breach of schools' legal duty to provide meals for pupils who want them.[42] Children have even been tricked into handing over their prints by being told they are going to play a 'game of spies' by the people entrusted to protect them.

From a young age, children are conditioned to give up their biometric data to further someone else's profit-driven whim, and 'to embrace the idea of Big Brother-style biometric tracking. If ever there was a generation that would not oppose a government system for universal ID, it's this one,' the US-based Electronic Privacy Information Center said in 2003. One York headteacher justified the stealthy fingerprinting of thousands of children across the city: 'All the measures to do with ID cards will possibly invade their privacy even further, but the world has no answer to terrorism without using these things and I would see us as getting them ready for the world in which they will have to live,' adding that parents had rarely complained.[43] It was more likely they didn't know, as the revelations only emerged via a Freedom of Information Act request.

Both the Irish Information Commissioner's Office and the Hong Kong Privacy Commissioner have slammed such practices, the former in 2007 deeming it unnecessary and in breach of the Data Protection Act to fingerprint children.[44] Fingerprinting may well also breach children's privacy as defined by Article 8 of the European Convention on Human Rights and Article 16 of the UN Convention on the Rights of the Child.[45]

What such technology can deliver is a false sense of security. In 2006, a Finnish military researcher revealed how fingerprints scanned by Microsoft's Fingerprint Reader, used for authenticating access to PCs since 2004, could be hacked and used for bogus authentication elsewhere. Microsoft had warned that the system was for convenience and not suitable for protecting sensitive data, but had the system's customers spent money on little more than a gimmick?[46] As ID management expert Andrew Clymer said: 'No system can guarantee the security of information against future technology. Attempting to protect lifetime relevant information is extremely tricky and potentially costly.'[47] Indeed, fingerprints can be recreated using latex or ballistics gel, or even photocopies, and have been proven to fool door scanners.[48]

A victim of fingerprint forgery cannot get new fingerprints, yet must live in a world where every daily transaction and function can depend on biometrics proving one's identity. Once those biometrics are compromised by criminals, a lifetime of inconvenience and false allegations can ensue. While commerce and government demand ever more intrusive biometric data in the name of mitigating risk, so the risks of data failure ruining people's lives increase. As IT security consultant Brian Drury said in 2007: 'If a child has never touched a fingerprint scanner, there is zero probability of being incorrectly investigated for a crime. Once a child has touched a scanner they will be at the mercy of the matching algorithm for the rest of their lives.'

There is also facial recognition technology in which

the distances between eyes, nose, mouth and cheek-bones are measured from digital video shots. Unlike fingerprint or iris scans, this can – when it works – be used at a distance, cameras homing in on particular subjects in a crowd without their being aware of it, let alone consenting. Still, the technology can be frustrated by the same problems that frustrated Bertillon – lighting, angle to camera, skin tone, beards, glasses or plastic surgery. A trial at Palm Beach International Airport in 2002 failed to identify employees 53 per cent of the time.

Vein patterns, also apparently unique to each person, are also being used for identification, and will be added to iris scans, photographs and, one day, DNA in the hope that their combined strength may overcome the deficiencies of one.[49] Some hope. A trial of the biometrics being tried for British ID cards, using over 2,000 volunteers, found that fingerprints did not work to verify almost a fifth of participants, and the devices were problematical for those 'with large fingers'. Facial scans only worked for 69 per cent of the group, and for 48 per cent of disabled volunteers. Iris scans fared well for most people but not for black or older participants. Some disabled people could not enroll using any of the systems.[50]

The technologies cannot be trusted to work – yet the authorities evidently have more faith in them than in the citizens they subject to suspicion. Every failure of technology is an opportunity for other devices that will enhance the ordering of humans by machines – those aiming to identify people by their palm, voice, writing style, typing speed, keystroke signatures or even their gait. German police even reprised the East German technique of sampling the sweat-stained cover of the seat upon which a suspect had been interrogated.

Progress in this field, as in many others, is not defined by proficiency, but by profit. Despite the economic downturn, the global biometric market is expected to grow at an annual rate of around 18 per cent between 2010 and 2012. North America and Europe had a 62-per-cent market share in 2009, with the market also growing rapidly in the Asia-Pacific region, where banks in particular are turning to biometrics to curb fraud and do away with PINs at ATMs.[51] US analysts Acuity Market Intelligence predict that, by 2017, Asia-Pacific will be the biggest biometric market with 32 per cent of global revenues, though markets in Central and South America are also growing at stellar annual rates of 39 per cent. Iris and facial recognition will compete with fingerprints by 2017.[52] The report notes the astounding projected growth of 61 per cent between 2009 and 2017 in the surveillance and monitoring sector, surging to $872 million in annual revenue. According to Acuity Principal C Maxine Most: 'Biometric Surveillance is the ultimate dream application of intelligence and defense communities and the waking nightmare of privacy and civil liberty advocates.'

DNA

The most personal biometric of all is DNA – Deoxyribonucleic acid – the unique code belonging to each human individual, which many in the surveillance world believe holds the key to a person's past, present and future. It is already the most trusted of all biometric identifiers – certainly the most potent, most personal and potentially the most violating.

Its use in tracking criminal suspects has been 'one of the biggest advances in tackling crime since fingerprinting', according to GeneWatch. The US's national DNA database has helped to investigate over 80,000 crimes since its inception. In a typical month in the UK, matches are found linking suspects to 30 murders, 45 rapes and 3,200 motor vehicle, property and drug crimes. DNA is vital to solving cold cases, bringing to justice those who have been too long at large, and solving gross miscarriages of justice: to date, 246 US inmates have been exonerated by DNA evidence, many having been in jail decades before DNA came into use.[53]

But DNA evidence can be misused by incompetents and abused, as with any other kind of evidence. In 2001, a US lab worker realized incorrect procedures had been used to eliminate DNA profiles from crime scene samples. Of over 100 samples revisited, one had been used in the conviction and sentencing of a man to 25 years for a rape he could not have committed. Or there was the DNA testing of the Omagh bomb debris that 'proved' the Northern Ireland bombing was carried out by a 14-year-old Nottingham schoolboy whose DNA was on the UK database as part of a paternity dispute. And DNA identification can be oversold. One US man was wrongly convicted of rape on the basis of a DNA sample and spent five years in jail, his DNA profile having been presented as belonging to only one in 700,000 black people, when it was really one in eight.[54] DNA can also be planted at crime scenes by perpetrators or investigators, and crime scenes may have many sources of DNA, or the samples be mislabeled, badly filed, inadvertently mixed or contaminated with DNA from elsewhere – in 2009, Britain's Cambridgeshire police were upbraided for storing DNA samples in a fridge alongside a chicken curry.

Ever since the establishment of the UK's National DNA Database, some have called for it to hold the DNA of everyone, innocent or not – in 1998, the élite National Crime Squad called for the DNA of every newborn baby to be taken.[55] Such calls have been resisted but laws have morphed over time to bring this practice closer to fruition. The 1984 Police and Criminal Evidence Act classed DNA as an 'intimate sample' to be taken only with consent for serious recordable offenses, with the sample destroyed if the arrestee was not charged, cautioned or was cleared. That was all binned with the 2001 Criminal Justice and Police Act, which allowed samples to be retained from those cleared of an offense or even if the charges were dropped. In addition, anyone outside the UK engaged in police work could speculatively trawl the national DNA database. The 2003 Criminal Justice Act then allowed police to take non-intimate samples without consent for any recordable offense at the point of arrest, with the data retained indefinitely even if the arrestee were never charged. Limits to when samples could be taken from juveniles or children were also watered down. By 2007, police were seeking powers for DNA sampling from suspects on the streets, for offenses such as speeding and littering.[56] Hence, by late 2008, the UK DNA database contained samples from 4,343,624 citizens, including hundreds of thousands of samples of wholly innocent people. In proportion to population this is the biggest DNA database in the world by far, and second in absolute terms only to the US's 6.54 million samples. By 2009, the number of children on the DNA database was 1.09 million, half of whom were innocent, and more than a third of these were under 16.[57] Yet the national DNA database is used annually, on average, in solving just 0.35 per cent of all crimes.[58]

The DNA database is more often used for racial profiling. Afro-Caribbeans comprise just 2.9 per cent of the UK population, but 27 per cent of the entire black population – and an astounding 40 per cent of black men – are on the DNA database, compared with just 6 per cent of the white population.[59] With nearly every black British family on the database, it is small wonder that there are doubts in the black community as to whether the Home Office and the police are the best custodians of black Britain's genetic heritage. Some argue that racial profiling could be remedied by having everyone's DNA on the database. But that would not stop racial profiling, just drown any evidence of it.[60]

The DNA database can also become a suspect list that results in people being turned down for jobs or visas, and which future governments could use to track individuals and their relatives: the Counter Terrorism Act 2008 allows the DNA database to be used to identify people, not just to solve crimes. These DNA samples may be used in research without people's consent, as happened with attempts to predict ethnicity based on DNA.

Sampling everybody would also worsen the risk of false matches, particularly among family members, and miscarriages of justice occurring as a result. With the uploading of incomplete samples to the database and individuals sharing profile traits, the chances of 'adventitious matches' occurring grows all the time,[61] and the number of false matches is expected to increase dramatically when DNA profiles are compared across the EU, beginning in 2011.[62]

In 2010, Sir Alex Jeffreys, the inventor of DNA fingerprinting, denounced to British MPs the storing of innocent people's DNA for its 'presumption of guilt' and related the story of one man's suicide which was linked to the retention of his DNA.[63] But the Home Office has consistently fought to keep all DNA records indefinitely – in defiance of its own citizens' inquiry that found innocent people's profiles should be deleted, and the European Court of Human Rights that ruled that such practices breached people's Article 8 right to privacy. In the US, the 1994 DNA Identification Act enabled the FBI to cross-match samples from the country's dozens of local and state databases, linked by the FBI-designed software, Combined DNA Index System (CODIS). From its dozen original members in 1994, CODIS had grown by 2009 to encompass over 170 public law enforcement agencies across all

50 states.

Most DNA databases were first built to deal with violent sexual crimes and homicides and the FBI genetically tracked only those previously convicted but, as in the UK, US laws were widened – more people became eligible for sampling, the severity of crimes qualifying for DNA inclusion was lowered and the point at which samples could be taken was brought forward.

The 2004 Justice for All Act allowed DNA to be uploaded for any felony – drug possession, car theft, burglary – and from suspects charged of any crime, even if the charges were dropped. The 2005 Violence Against Women Act, amended with the DNA Fingerprint Act, meant that arrestees no longer needed to be charged for their DNA to be uploaded, and the acquitted had to provide certified proof of charges being dismissed, a bureaucratic hoop making the retention of the sample much more likely. The Federal collection of DNA from non-US citizens from immigration and border agencies followed. Although differences between Federal and state law do exist, the laws are converging.

By 2008, CODIS had been used in some 80,948 investigations and offender profiles had risen to 6,539,919 from 460,365 in 2000. The FBI hopes that more money and laws will 'dramatically' increase the annual number of new DNA entries from 80,000 to 1.2 million by 2012, inevitably also increasing the backlog of DNA data being processed, already estimated at half a million profiles by mid-2009.[64] CODIS's non-criminal usage is, moreover, being expanded to include enhanced kinship analysis software so as to identify missing and unidentified persons and their relatives.

The falling cost of DNA technology has made gene screening a booming private business, with firms such as Navigenics, Knome and Iceland's DeCode Genetics cashing in on burgeoning public interest in genealogy.[65] The US has no federal law about 'abandoned DNA', so in 2008 the remains of a breakfast supposedly eaten by President Obama ended up on eBay with Obama's DNA supposedly on the silverware. It seems anybody's DNA can be found and sold.

There was the alleged newspaper plot in 2002 to steal hair from the British royal family's Prince Harry and test whether he was really the son of Princess Diana's lover James Hewitt. In 2007, the French government approved the DNA testing of immigrants seeking to prove they have family in the country, advised by the International Organization for Migration, which has collected thousands of samples from migrants seeking to live in Australia, Italy, Britain and the US.[66]

The US-based firm Beta Genetics offers various DNA-screening tests to trace lineage and relations, or help make a patron 'a happy father without any doubts'. Beta Genetics makes it a selling-point that 13 of the 16 DNA markers used in its tests are the 'core CODIS markers', more pointedly showing the technological convergence between the public sectors of law enforcement and private business. Google start-up 23andMe seeks to help 'consumers understand and browse their genome'.[67] The tobacco, chemical and nuclear industries have vested interests in promoting the idea of genetic susceptibility and shifting blame for disease away from bad products or pollution and onto bad genes.[68] The US's first court case of genetic discrimination came in 2002 when Burlington Northern Santa Fe Corp was fined millions of dollars for illegally testing 36 workers who had claimed that their work induced carpal tunnel syndrome, in an attempt to prove that they were actually just genetically predisposed.[69] Biopharma industries profit from selling genetic tests that predict common diseases and then selling 'preventive' medicines to the 'worried well', which, if done through state health services, would leave scant resources for treating the poor and sick.[70] Anti-discrimination laws notwithstanding, 'bad' DNA would undoubtedly impact on some people's job prospects and income, and their own DNA could become a source of debilitating stress.

By 1998, New Zealand, France and Australia had all set up their own DNA databases, with Canada following in 2000. China has also set one up to track the thousands of missing children lost to human trafficking – a worthy intent, but other uses for the data will inevitably follow. While most national databases have not yet followed up the International Association of Police Chiefs' 1999 call for the world's police forces to take DNA upon arrest for any crime, the global sharing of DNA is fast becoming realized, as the G8 justice and interior ministers have long sought.[71] CODIS is used by over 40 law-enforcement laboratories in over 25 countries, and is compatible with Interpol's new DNA Gateway, which will share DNA data between states under the 2005 Prüm Treaty.

While the Danes have been taking the DNA of their babies at birth since 1981 to test for diseases and later for finding criminals, Tony Blair's suggestion that the UK should do the same provoked uproar – as did New York mayor Rudolf Giuliani's similar proposal. Maybe it's because Danish parents can have the blood sample destroyed after use for disease screening – or maybe the Danes just trust their government more.

1 Walter Dornberger, *V-2*, Ballantine, 1954. 2 Global CCTV Market Analysis (2008-2012) http://nin.tl/a5K3u8 3 Henry Porter, *Suspect Nation*, Channel 4 TV, 2006. 4 Expert Findings on Surveillance Cameras, ACLU, 2008. 5 *The Wharf*, 5 July 2007. 6 UK Home Office, *The impact of CCTV: 14 case studies*, 2005, rds. homeoffice.gov.uk/rds/pdfs05/rdsolr1505.pdf 7 Brendan O'Neill, 'Watching you, watching me', *New Statesman*, 2 Oct 2006. 8 'Talking CCTV scolds offenders', BBC news, 4 April 2007. 9 http://bit.ly/adGC85 10 ACLU, Bigger Monster, Weaker Chains, 2003. 11 UK Home Office, op cit. 12 Facial Recognition Technology (FERET) database http://nin.tl/bhJWSw 13 'Interpol wants facial recognition database to catch suspects', *The Guardian*, 20 Oct 2008. 14 Henry Porter, 'Privacy is not a needle in a haystack', *The Guardian*, 14 May 2009.

http://nin.tl/bl6gBY 15 http://nin.tl/dC5CE0 16 'Train station to get terrorist-tracking CCTV', *Daily Telegraph*, 27 Jun 2007. 17 'The tiny airline spy that spots bombers in the blink of an eye', *Daily Mail*, 12 Feb 2007. 18 http://nin.tl/aYJnoh 19 http://nin.tl/cpBJbe 20 *The Guardian*, 23 Jan 2010 http://nin.tl/a9HwwQ 21 Katherine Albrecht & Liz McIntyre, *Spychips*, Nelson, 2005. 22 Electronic Privacy Information Center http://epic.org/privacy/rfid 23 Niniek Karmini, 'Microchips for AIDS patients in eastern Indonesia', Associated Press, 24 Nov 2008. 24 'US state turns to RFID to monitor inmates', *Computerworld*, 19 Jun 2007. 25 Celeste Biev, 'Plan to chip Alzheimer's patients causes protest', *New Scientist* 19 May 2007. 26 www.antichips.com/cancer/index.html 27 Do Chip Implants Protect or Violate Privacy? ABC, 18 May 2007. 28 http://nin.tl/9Dv5Jx 29 http://nin.tl/aoDPpx 30 *Metro*, 26 Nov 2007. 31 http://nin.tl/dvHvMz 32 *Spychips*, op cit. 33 http://nin.tl/d9RGF6 34 http://nin.tl/9HwGAw 35 http://nin.tl/cjp6to 36 Simon Burns, 6 March 2008, v3.co.uk/articles/print/2211418 37 Bernard S Cohn 'Colonialism and its forms of knowledge: The British in India', Princeton, 1996. 38 Christian Parenti, *The Soft Cage*, Basic Books, 2003. 39 'FBI apology for Madrid bomb fingerprint fiasco', *The Register*, 26 May 2004. 40 The global deployment of biometrics can be read up on at the industry news filter, www.findbiometrics.com 41 *The Register*, 4 May 2005. http://nin.tl/8YOyoQ 42 *The Register*, 4 Oct 2007 http://nin.tl/9sgo9T 43 *The Press*, 8 Jan 2007 http://nin.tl/agmIWj 44 *The Register* 23 March 2007 http://nin.tl/cxquud 45 http://nin.tl/dblaov 46 IDG News, 6 Mar 2006, http://nin.tl/bun1RW 47 Do Biometrics have a role for school registration? http://nin.tl/a9WRUl 48 Mythbusters episode 59, Discovery Channel. 49 http://nin.tl/cOwnQM 50 BBC 25 May 2005 http://nin.tl/aWhvMm 51 http://nin.tl/bMjToE 52 Biometric surveillance forecast, 8 Sep 2009 www.findbiometrics.com/articles/i/7275/ 53 BBC, 18 Dec 2009, http://nin.tl/c3oO8g 54 Genewatch, http://nin.tl/d526CL 55 http://nin.tl/ax3oaZ 56 *The Times online*, http://nin.tl/aKCLoK 57 http://nin.tl/aQ8BG4 58 Gareth Crossman, 'Overlooked: Surveillance and personal privacy in Modern Britain', Liberty, 2007. 59 Matilda MacAttram, http://nin.tl/bdxNEf. 60 Tania Simoncelli, ACLU, http://nin.tl/b8Sofl 61 Henry Porter, *The Guardian* blog, 29 May 2009, citing genetic researcher and lawyer Brian Costello. 62 GeneWatch, http://nin.tl/doBNYN 63 *Daily Telegraph*, 4 Feb 2010. 64 *New York Times*, 18 Apr 2009 http://nin.tl/bBCv2z 65 'Who's testing your DNA?' *New Scientist*, 24 Jan 2009. 66 *New York Times*, 15 Nov 2007 http://nin.tl/cXVKl2 67 Kevin Kelleher, http://nin.tl/cicDW 68 Genewatch http://nin.tl/9Ka9Cz 69 Reuters, 8 May 2002, http://nin.tl/bKGUpkm 70 Genewatch http://nin.tl/9Ka9Cz 71 http://nin.tl/an9L1V

6 Big Brother is watching – and making a fat profit

We are now subject to routine surveillance – in our workplaces, through our medical records, through our computer use – to an extent that would have been thought impossible in the West a generation ago. And governments are being pushed ever further down this road to Big Brother by an increasingly powerful array of security corporations.

The British firm ACLCamCom's website reminds its corporate customers that CCTV can help ensure that minimum-waged workers don't spend too long smoking or chatting with friends.[1] Meanwhile, the US firm Diversified Risk Management offers undercover and covert operations, investigations into substance abuse, accidents, worker compensation fraud and IT security, employing 'night-vision generation 3 lenses, GPS, and wireless recording systems' to get hits.[2] Indian businesses can be served by the Delhi-based National Detectives & Corporate Consultants. DIY snoops can kit out at www.spyequipmentguide.com, www.spygearsite.com, www.brickhousesecurity.com, www.spyworld.com, and buy camera-pens and long-range recording devices for use in the office.

Hewlett Packard board members' telephone records were hacked by private investigators hired by their own company, which wanted to find out which executive was leaking information to which journalist. A New York school carpenters' supervisor was fired for leaving work early, his employers having tracked his movements through his GPS-installed mobile phone. While he fought his case and was reinstated, many employees prefer just to leave such poisonous work environments.

Workplace surveillance is both good for business and is big business. Industrialization brought the masses under surveillance, with factories imposing a regimen of time-keeping and shiftwork on workforces of recently uprooted rural folk. People were broken up into units of production as quantifiable as – and far more disposable than – the machines and products they tended. Mass production theories like Taylorism and Fordism were adopted wholesale by all domains – capitalist, communist and fascist.

The march to modernity now demands that chimneys be replaced with towers made of concrete, steel and glass, housing service industries. From the point of accessing the building past the security guard and his array of CCTV screens, workers enter through pass-activated gates and into designated, pass-enabled work areas. Within open-plan workspaces, glass-walled meeting rooms flank rows of low-walled cubicles, the essence of panoptical surveillance that ensures maximum productivity. CCTV monitors the work floors. All internal and external emails and instant messaging can be monitored in real-time and retained for later use, with every website visited on your browser logged and unacceptable websites blocked. Phones might not be bugged, but software exists – 'unified messaging' – to convert audio calls into text and dispatch the data by email, rendering it subject to different data retention laws.[3] What is done on company property is company property and there is nothing that can be deleted from an office computer, BlackBerry or voicemail that cannot be remotely retrieved.

In-house card-catering schemes for use in the canteen and in vending machines enable firms to monitor employees' diet, and the frequency of use of the subsidized gym or washrooms, indicating possible time-wasting, drug abuse, or some health problem (frequent urination possibly indicating diabetes, say).

Big Brother is watching

The iHygiene product monitors the handwashing habits of RFID-tagged employees during bathroom visits.

Reference checking beyond the narrow, biased scope of those suggested by the candidate was once a tortuous task for bosses, which in the modern age created a lucrative niche for private, impartial companies able to screen candidates. The Society for Human Resource Management found that 51 per cent of companies used screening firms to carry out such checks in 1996; by 2004, 96 per cent of them were doing so, with long-standing employees also being screened. By 2008, candidate screening had developed into a $4-billion industry in the US alone, with the market led by ChoicePoint and USIS, supported by others like Experian or Kroll. Their services are sought to vet Starbucks' baristas and Wal-Mart shelf-stackers by sifting through, for example, credit records, criminal records, driving records, education records, court records, bankruptcy, neighbor interviews, military records, sex offender lists, prison records, drug test records, past employers' records and, in some US states, medical records.[4]

Criminal records and credit checks are standard, but call-center staff also phone former employers, colleagues and friends to enquire about work habits, personal character, drug or alcohol problems, beefing out these digi-dossiers with any number of unsubstantiated claims and allegations. One background-checking company reminds employers that they face great risks from potential employees: 'Are they really who they say they are?... Are they really financially stable? Do they have a criminal record?' Failing to check supposedly exposes your firm to fraud, data theft, high staff turnover levels and negligence suits. Nonetheless, the scrutiny industry is itself not very well scrutinized – the president of one major firm said the business was as unregulated as the 'wild, wild West', with no great emphasis on compliance or on hiring high-quality people to do the screening.[5]

The public sector is no better. In 2009, French data protection agency CNIL reported that up to a million people had either lost jobs or did not get them due to inaccuracies in the French criminal record check system, the Système de Traitement des Infractions Constatés, created in 1995 but not acknowledged until 2001. Meanwhile, two more French police databases were created in 2008: CRISTINA, pertaining to defense, was to be classified, while EDVIGE proposed to hold data on citizens' political or union affiliations, religious beliefs, and information on anyone above the age of 13 considered a 'suspect' capable of disrupting public order. Nationwide demonstrations spiked CRISTINA, while EDVIGE's fate is unknown, but police access the Système some 20 million times a year, despite an error rate of 83 per cent. Alleged offenses continue to be uploaded while court decisions, including acquittals, are not. Suspects remain suspects.[6]

In the UK, the Consulting Association's database served dozens of UK construction industry firms for 15 years with the personal details, work histories, union activity, political leanings and personal relationships of over 3,200 workers, all of whom were oblivious to the database's existence. The Information Commissioner's Office closed it down in 2008[7] – just when the perfectly legitimate National Staff Dismissal Register went online, supported by the UK Home Office and British Retail consortium, Harrods and Reed Managed Services. This register was replete with uninvestigated allegations of stealing, fraud or damaging company property, even if no prosecutions ensued or the 'accused' resigned before facing disciplinary proceedings. Employers can still do their own detective work in their bedrooms – an estimated 45 per cent of employers trawl social networking sites, to 'learn more' about job candidates, with Facebook being the 'site of choice'[8] and a third rejecting candidates who complain about former employers, have dodgy photographs or chat about drugs.[9] Current employees can also suffer through Facebook monitoring. Teenager Kimberley Swann was fired by Ivell Marketing & Logistics for describing her job as 'boring' on her Facebook page, even though she did not name the company.[10]

Workers under constant monitoring suffer higher stress rates. A survey by the UK Policy Studies Institute found that admin and white-collar employees whose emails, internet usage and keystrokes were logged, and whose calls were recorded and timed, suffered a 10-per-cent increase in stress, while semi-skilled and manual workers reported an 8-per-cent increase.[11] This is a problem for which another techno-solution may exist, such as Microsoft's patent for the use of wireless sensors linked to computers to measure workers' heart rate, respiration rate, body temperature, facial movements and brain signals. When conjoined with workers' psychological profiles and data on their weight, age and health, managers could be remotely informed of levels of frustration or stress, and help or dismiss accordingly.[12] Employers could thus achieve higher productivity, or, better still, avoid lawsuits if workers suffer stress, while workers would undergo Winston Smith's battle to never let his face display his disdain for his work to the camera on his desk in *Nineteen Eighty-Four*.

Medical records

Totalitarian regimes do not only execute, imprison or 'disappear' dissidents. Sometimes dictators seek to be more benevolent and 're-educate' those deluded fools who must be mentally ill if they think they know better than the Party or the State. From the 1930s, Soviet dissidents were incarcerated in NKVD-run mental hospital-prisons, *psikushkas*, becoming psychiatric guinea-pigs in which Nurse Ratchetska could treat their paranoia about living in an oppressive state. If they were not mentally disturbed on arrival, they would soon become so in a world where no fool could take their ramblings about 'freedom' seriously. Russia's medical profession was so repelled by its own collusion with abuses of psychiatry that within months of the USSR's collapse it had confessed to all and by 1992 Russia had signed into law a new core of psychiatric practices and patients' rights modeled on US medical practice.[13]

But Nurse Ratchet was of course American, where that same year, the ugliest example of exploiting the stigma of mental illness for political ends surfaced. Nydia Velázquez won the nomination to represent the Democratic Party in one of New York City's Congressional seat races. But just weeks into the candidate's campaign, the *New York Post* phoned her to say that every city newspaper was to give front-page treatment to the story of her attempted suicide a year before. Someone at St Claire's Hospital, where Velázquez was treated, had faxed her medical notes to the papers about her depressed act of despair. Velázquez bravely countered with a pre-emptive press conference and her would-be constituents accepted she was restored to full health and control – at the time of writing, she is still in the House of Representatives. The medical records of the late Farrah Fawcett and Maria Shriver, wife of California governor Arnold Schwarzenegger, were among 61 patients' files that were 'improperly accessed' by an employee at UCLA Medical Center,[14] while Britney Spears is another of countless celebrities or politicos whose records have been made public. But this kind of tabloid titillation is just the ingrown toenail of the tumor-ridden body that is profit from medical data.

The perception among Americans that what they

tell their doctor is private and that their data will be disclosed only with their permission, is false. Indeed they may never know when their records are accessed, or by whom.[15] The US hosts a vast industry devoted to sifting and selling medical data, hubbed by the Medical Information Bureau. This group seeks to protect the 470-odd US and Canadian insurance companies that operate it from 'attempts to conceal or omit information material to the sound and equitable underwriting of life, health, disability, income, critical illness and long-term care insurance'. This is done by selling data to life and health insurance companies, brokers, transcription vendors, employers, credit bureaus and banks. Credit ratings and cholesterol scores share the same file space because good health means good credit – dying people default on their debts. One banker also sat on his county's health board and, having crosschecked customer accounts with patient information, called in the mortgages of everyone suffering from cancer.[16] US law allows private health insurers to deny consumers insurance if they have pre-existing, prohibitively expensive long-term conditions, with one in ten applicants failing at the preliminary screening, sometimes based on data about ailments their grandparents endured.[17]

The risk of damning patients to fatally expensive health premiums has led some doctors to record ailments and billing codes using code 'surrogate' terms such as 'adjustment disorder' instead of 'depression'. But insurance companies second-guess such codes and infer that 'generalized anxiety' may really mean the costlier condition of depression, and raise premiums accordingly.

Every condition profits pharmaceutical firms and costs insurers, so the Medical Marketing Service sells lists of persons, cross-referenced with information ranging from education and family dwelling size to lifestyle and children, suffering anything from psoriasis to hyperthyroidism, constipation to dandruff, cancer and impotence. Marketing firms make eerie use of such data. A woman bought fertility drugs at a San Diego pharmacy. While her efforts to have a baby were all in vain, that purchase delivered her personal details to a marketing system and, like a modern Lieutenant Kizhe (the Russian officer invented by a bureaucrat's mistake), a marketing algorithm gave birth to a paper baby that led to a decade's worth of junk mail from Pampers and promotional gifts for an elementary school graduate, all shadowing the life of the child who never was.[18]

Already, though, the 1996 Health Insurance Portability and Accountability Act had incinerated patient privacy, wherein simply 'asserting that you are a suspect of the victim of a crime' meant law enforcement officials could access medical files without a warrant – not that the suspect need ever know about it.[19] The Act also allows information to be divulged not just by your health provider, but by pharmacies, health clearinghouses, medical research facilities and various medical associations. Section 215 of the Patriot Act, moreover, allows the FBI to sift data about people's piles in order to fight terrorism. One US company sought to sell its face-recognition-enabled CCTV by adding data on students' medical histories and medications. Thus anyone suspected of homicidal tendencies seen walking onto campus or into a school would be identifiable by security staff and intercepted. Which conditions and medications exactly lead people to mass murder is not clear, so everyone suffering depression can be assured that they will be suspected.

Computerized medical records trump paper ones that are expensive to store and only exist in immovable locations. But paper records are advantageous for confidentiality, whereas electronic data can – and does – beam worldwide at the speed of light and, as the US National Research Council warned, makes the data prey to insiders who access and disseminate such data, by accident, incompetence, curiosity, spite or for criminal gain.

In 2009, computer hackers ransomed the state of Virginia for $10 million for 8 million patient records and 35 million prescriptions stolen from the state's prescription drug database.[20] The boss of an Indian outsourcing company, meanwhile, was arrested for selling hundreds of confidential medical records, with names, addresses and phone numbers, of patients treated at one of Britain's top private hospitals – he had hawked them via internet chatrooms for as little as $6 each.[21] Laptops containing the unencrypted records of 7,000 NHS Birmingham patients were stolen;[22] East Cheshire NHS Trust was upbraided after sensitive patient data was found dumped in skips;[23] while City and Hackney Primary Care Trust confessed to the loss of a disc containing data on 160,000 children.[24]

In any event, citizens of England and Wales are having their 'confidential' medical details uploaded to a national database called SPINE, along with a pithy Summary Care Record version, noting allergies or long-standing conditions, and name, address and phone numbers. When the database is fully operational, these details will be accessible to NHS staff, pharmacists, civil servants and social workers – anything up to a million government employees. Doctors and civil servants can override requests to opt out of the system, including refusing services to opted-out patients.

Technical problems and costs exceeding £12 billion ($18 billion) have held up SPINE, but the government seeks to make the system pay for itself by selling its data. Already, the Health and Social Care Act 2001 gives the Secretary of State the power to invent data regulations as per the processing of patient information for medical purposes as deemed 'necessary or expedient' – including selling it. A surreptitious

The booming market in surveillance

CCTV

2009   **$13 billion**
2014   **$28 billion**

In 2006, North America and Europe accounted for 85% of the global CCTV market. But Asia is expected to be the dominant region by 2012, with 45% of the market.

Sources: http://nin.tl/9smdAr & http://nin.tl/92h9Xl

ID documents and cards

2009   **$5.8 billion**
2014   **$10.3 billion**

Growth sectors will be e-passports, ID cards, credit cards, transit cards and driving licenses, with the financial sectors leading the push.

Source: http://nin.tl/9lDegb

Biometrics

2009   **$3.4 billion**
2014   **$9.4 billion**

Automated fingerprint, iris, face, vein and voice recognition technologies.

Sources: http://nin.tl/bTleP4 & http://nin.tl/di1kSt

RFIDS

2009   **$5.5 billion**
2014   **$10.7 billion**

Radio Frequency Identifiers, mainly to be used in retail, e-passports and Chinese ID cards.

Source: http://nin.tl/9ha4Wq

clause in the 2009 Coroners and Justice Bill sought to give insurance companies, research organizations and government departments unlimited access to medical data without patients' consent. The clause was removed in the face of protests – however, it's anyone's guess how and when such a heist may be tried again.

Patients' medical data isn't really theirs and their consent over its dissemination – which is fundamental to the relationship of trust between doctor and patient – is not needed. NHS staff priorities have been re-engineered to emphasize their loyalties to their employers, the state. UK medical staff must report to police any gunshot and knife victims as well as any children who have suffered any kind of accidental cut. Doctors may also breach confidentiality if they suspect a crime has happened, or will happen. Further, the UK's General Medical Council has adjusted medical staff operating guidelines to allow family members to be informed of someone's affliction with an inherited condition, even if the person does not wish it disclosed.[25] Doctors are also to report patients with defective eyesight to the Driver Vehicle Licensing Agency. Doctors may become quicker to condemn so as to protect themselves from potential lawsuits, and patients far slower to see them, to their own detriment.

Would visitors to sexual health clinics still be guaranteed anonymity? If not, the possible impacts might include increased insurance premiums or being judged unsuitable to work with children. The same might apply to those seeking treatment for drink or drug abuse, particularly as it may affect entitlements to state benefits. And doctors are sometimes the only people in whom rape victims can confide – would they do so if they thought there was any possibility of global disclosure? As the British Medical Association says: 'If patients cannot be 100-per-cent sure that their records are confidential, they will inevitably be reluctant to share vital information with their doctor.'[26]

Aiding repression

Governments and the private sector have long co-operated in surveillance.[27] The US Secret Service was created neither to help douse the embers of the Civil War nor to protect the soon-to-be-murdered President Lincoln, but to stop currency counterfeiting. Meanwhile private 'detective' agencies such as Pinkertons, which failed to protect Lincoln from assassination, did much better helping 19th-century American employers battle their disgruntled workers and unions. And then there were the 'corporate

Drug tests and teddy bears

The widespread practice of companies testing employees for drug abuse (80 per cent of US companies now do this[1]) originated from a fatal US Navy plane crash in 1981 that exposed widespread drug abuse among US Navy personnel. Drug testing was introduced across the armed services, then for all civil and Federal workers in safety-sensitive jobs, before spilling into the private sector under the 1988 Drug Free Workplace Act.

Soon enough the concept was extended to have anyone on state benefits prove drug abuse was not behind their enforced idleness. In 1994, New York mayor Rudy Giuliani failed in his attempt to have all single, childless people on benefits undergo a medical exam and drug test,[2] but the UK's Department of Work and Pensions took up this idea in 2009, getting claimants to complete questionnaires about their drug or alcohol use and lose their benefits if enough boxes were ticked by staff (who themselves probably had claim-reduction targets to meet) or if they refused the test.[3]

Other fraud-fighting innovations from Britain's Department of Work and Pensions have included Clive, the CCTV-equipped teddy bear, designed to be given to benefit claimants' children so that they could unwittingly film their supposedly fraudulent parents in their homes. The Department has also adopted insurance industry tactics, such as using voice stress analysis equipment – lie detectors – to identify people phoning in a fraudulent claim.[4] In 2010 an Australian billboard campaign exhorting workers to 'dob' their mates if suspected of benefit fraud was proposed for the UK, with informers to get a cut of any benefits saved.[5] ∎

1 http://nin.tl/b95gz9 2 *New York Times*, 17 Nov 1994, http://nin.tl/9m9jmE 3 *The Observer*, 27 Sep 2009, http://nin.tl/9a91pN 4 BBC news, 27 Jan 2005, http://nin.tl/aNCiGR 5 *The Guardian*, 8 Feb 2010, http://nin.tl/aMWMhO

officials, labor spies, super-patriots, amateur detectives and assorted vigilantes' who worked with the government to combat radicalism after World War One and remained active in various forms right through to the last years of the Cold War.

Just as Western Union had to comply with US censorship laws and hand over all the telegrams to the government, so Yahoo! argued that it gave the Chinese police the data they needed to arrest and jail human-rights journalist Shi Tao in 2005 because the company had to comply with the law. But does complying with the law mean being a police informant? Did Microsoft have to remove Chinese blogs criticising Beijing? Was Cisco compelled to sell its hardware to build China's Great Firewall (see page 152)? Did MSN have to carry photos of wanted Tibetan protestors on its news portal, or Sky scan its Chinese-language users' chat messaging for keywords like 'democracy' and copy the results to the company's servers?[28] Google's belated attempt not to be evil in early 2010, when it threatened to stop censoring its Chinese search engine after frequent hacks, drew a derisory snort from Bill Gates: 'Do you want to obey the laws of the countries you're in or not? If not, you may not end up doing business there.'[29] And if the laws happen to be those of a police state, and helping to sniff out dissidents is profitable, well... bad luck.

In states where there is theoretically more redress against such malevolent governance, it makes sense for governments to privatize or outsource its surveillance. This enables governments to access private-sector databases which usually hold way more data than the government could otherwise accumulate (most people work in and transact with private businesses far more than they do with the state, and often give – willingly or unwittingly – much more data to private companies than they would to governments).

When the state cannot find the path of least resistance to avoiding privacy laws, then it can legislate to gather the data from systems built and maintained by the private sector – like the internet or telephone systems. That way, it gets the private sector to pay for the cost of compliance, as with the requirement to retain all internet data for several months, or with phone companies being forced by the FBI to follow particular specifications so as to enable wiretapping (see page 55).[30] The customer always pays in the end, anyway. And the co-opted private firm can share the blame if the surveillance is rumbled. Hence, for very little financial outlay or bad publicity, governments can massively expand their spying, collating 1,000 private sources into one almighty collage for trawling by data-mining algorithms.

Uncertainty over what information can be gleaned by the government, and by what means, can enormously amplify the effect of government surveillance on individual behavior and psychology.

Military spin-offs

Many a military development has had a civilian spin-off benefit. The internet itself derived from the works of the spooky US government think-tank RAND and the Defense Department's Advanced Research Project Agency (DARPA) to build a data-distributing 'net' that could not be incapacitated by singular atomic bombs. Much of the internet was built and paid for by corporate surveillance of its users, as websites placed unique identifier 'cookie' files on users' computer hard-drives to enable marketing companies such as DoubleClick to track users' browsing habits and amass personality profiles on a scale that the FBI could only envy. 'Free' email services and software like RealAudio persuaded users to give up their invaluable data for 'free' for software firms to hoover up and sell. Numerous software and hardware packages facilitate wholesale monitoring of data traffic circulating within and without a company, carrying out tasks like the dubiously termed 'package sniffing', as algorithms seek out dodgy keywords and phrases in emails. IT staff have their own codified language of power over other employees that reveals itself through acronyms: IDS (intrusion detection systems), SIM (security information management) and CMS (central monitoring system).[31]

The civilian-military symbiosis is two-way, however. Thus Google sells its server technology and software to US intelligence agencies building Intellipedia, US spooks' closed equivalent of Wikipedia. Similarly, credit-rating algorithms are being adapted for use in data-mining for terrorist suspects. The CIA would love to have data-mining technologies that would allow it to monitor and profile potential terrorists as closely and carefully as Amazon monitors and profiles potential customers.[32]

It is hoped that the tech boom being fostered by the investment in the security and surveillance businesses, in which cumulative private and public sector security spending in the US is alone forecast to exceed $1 trillion between 2005 and 2015, may lead to another bonanza in civilian spin-offs. 'The money flowing into military and homeland infrastructure security will leverage revolutionary technologies and materials of the new digital age,' according to *Forbes*, with innovative strides made in medicine, industry, telecoms and entertainment arising from the work of entrepreneurs not only battling terror but also facilitating economies of scale. Sensors that sniff potential chemical weapons could improve environmental monitoring, medical imaging would benefit from developing scanners to see through packages, radar for monitoring perimeters and borders could enhance truck safety.

The big guns of General Electric, Northrop Grumman and Lockheed Martin long ago realized that bombs and rockets are not the be-all and end-all – the post-Cold War 'peace' would need the subtler technologies and services of security and, besides, a more secure world would need fewer bombs.

Hence Lockheed Martin has branched out into municipal social and civil-service programs across the US for many years, its tentacles reaching into pies ranging from parking enforcement, toll collection and CCTV traffic camera systems to welfare-to-work programs (in which large corporations receive shipments of government-subsidized workers who lose their welfare unless they work for minimum wages) and tracking child support payments.

The security-industrial complex

Back in 1961, Republican President 'Ike' Dwight Eisenhower warned in his parting speech: 'In the councils of government, we must guard against the acquisition of unwarranted influence, whether sought or unsought, by the military-industrial complex. The potential for the disastrous rise of misplaced power exists and will persist.' The influence of the immense military establishment and arms industry is, he went on, 'felt in every city, every State house, every office of the Federal government' and its existence presented an epic opportunity cost, with funding for schools, hospitals, and homeless people instead going on bombs and rockets. But by the 21st century, such a terrifying entity was widely seen as good for the economy, and therefore as a good thing in its own right. As *Forbes* cheered in 2004, 'a security-industrial complex is rapidly emerging, echoing its military kissing-cousin,' and there were huge benefits to be had from all the capital flows, innovation and profit that would ensue – including the rescue of Silicon Valley from its post-dot.com bubble-bust.

Ike was 'hardly a renowned left-wing firebrand', as the then British Home Secretary John Reid told a conference of security system manufacturers in 2006. Reid scoffed that the UK government would not be so naïve as to fall for any military-industrial-security complex, indeed, 'perhaps we are fortunate that the size of today's budgets and the competitiveness of markets may make Eisenhower's fears less relevant today.' Reid said he was struck by the UK Security and Resilience Supply Base's observation that the UK market in security and resilience was fragmented and its budgets too small. 'Your emerging trade body's suggestion that links are established with ministerial leaders and wider stakeholders seems in keeping with my insistence that everyone is involved in the struggle to advance our values. On these terms I would be keen to see how universities, trade unions and the voluntary sector are able to contribute too.'

Eisenhower's vision of Federal domination by employment and research grants of 'the free university, historically the fountainhead of free ideas and scientific discovery' was already apparent, with government contracts virtually substituting for intellectual curiosity. Reid's government was happy to help grow the UK's surveillance industry into a world player, making it integral to Britain's economy, society, academia and government.[33]

Stiff overseas competition was already arising, with the Pentagon spending tens of billions of dollars per year on research and development, much of it going into security research at university level and private start-ups. Not to be outdone, Europe's arms and security firms lobbied for EU funding. In 2003, a 'Group of Personalities', comprising EU officials and Europe's biggest arms and IT companies, agreed that European transnationals were 'losing out' to their US competitors and their billion-dollar government R&D grants, and so the EU Security Research Program was created – 'Big Brother meets market fundamentalism', as Ben Hayes of Statewatch phrased it. The European Commission gave the group 'a seat at the EU table, a proposed budget of one billion euros for "security" research and all but full control over the development and implementation of the program'. The companies were not only to build the products, they were to direct the security policies that would purchase and deploy them. At a stroke they would be safeguarding the EU's citizens, safeguarding their own funding and safeguarding Brussels' power through the technology and policies of oppression – all of this without debate.[34]

The Seventh Framework for Research 2007-2013

lists 45 cryptically titled projects, like COPE and CRESCENDO and SAMURAI, to the uglier iDetecT 4ALL. The organizations involved are being paid to find problems, invent solutions and devise their application. The project for the Automatic Detection of Abnormal Behaviour and Threats (ADABTs) in crowded Spaces illustrates how the system reaches across the borderless EU into every stratum of business, government and universities. It involves the UK's BAe Systems and the Home Office Scientific Development Branch, Norway's Detec A/S, Holland's military R&D institute and the University of Amsterdam, Sweden's Totalforsvarets Forskningsinstitut, with input from Bulgaria's Institute of Psychology.

Globalization means that any private firm can win any contract anywhere from out sourcing governments. US company LM, which is big in biometrics and space lasers, has also run censuses for the US and Canada, and is set to run the 2011 UK Census for the UK's Office of National Statistics. The UK government said it was 'pretty confident' the data gathered by the Census would remain secure but the US Patriot Act allows the US government and intelligence agencies to sequester any personal data taken by US companies, without anyone's consent. LM's involvement in the 2006 Canadian Census deterred many Canadians from participating, resulting in incomplete data, skewed statistics and wonky policies.

The revolving door of private commerce, the military and government whirs until it blurs. DARPA's Total Information Awareness program was originally proposed by the Syntek company, of which DARPA director John Poindexter was vice-president. Former Secretary of Homeland Security Tom Ridge claimed in 2005 that RFIDs in US passports would 'make us safer' – he was at the time a director of RFID-maker Savi Technology.[35] Former UK Home Secretary David Blunkett often used his column in *The Sun* newspaper

to champion the need for ID cards, not mentioning
that he was a consultant to the Texas-based ID maker,
Entrust.[36] Former Homeland Security chief Michael
Chertoff publicly proclaimed the need for full body
scanners at US airports, which would have been of
great benefit to scanner-maker RapiScan, a client of
his lobby firm, Chertoff Group.[37] Biometrics special-
ists L-1's rapid securing of over a billion dollars of
US government contracts was, of course, unrelated to
the fact that CIA director George Tenet was a board
member.

ECHELON – the joint signals intelligence unit
operated by Australia, Canada, New Zealand, the UK
and the US (see page 40) – is also used for commercial
interests, to earn its way in the world and to profit
its backers. One German MEP has claimed European
businesses have lost over 20 billion euros ($28 billion)
due to ECHELON's interceptions being used to
pip the competition – as when McDonnell-Douglas
scooped a $6-billion deal with the Saudis over the
French and Airbus, while Raytheon muscled in with a
share of a $1.3-billion radar deal between Brazil and
a French radar company.

The EU's need for ECHELON-proof communications partly inspired the work on its 30-strong
constellation of Galileo surveillance satellites,
bequeathing Brussels a Global Positioning System
independent of the dominant US version and allowing
EU military forces to act independently of Washington.
A tatty EU video explains the benefits of this system
to European taxpayers, including the disappearance
of motorway toll queues (car-borne GPS allowing
individual drivers to pay-per-kilometer) and iPhone
functions such as finding the nearest restaurant. More
pointedly, the precise locating of all people and things
would transform governance, according to the chief
executive of Nottingham Scientific Ltd, Professor
Vidal Ashkenazil: 'Just like time at present governs

the lives of ordinary citizens, so will position and its instant communication to others' – the question of exactly who is governing those lives and in whose interests is left aside.

Surveillance is not just seen as a tool for running the country more efficiently, or for scoring an advantage over a competitor without recourse to war, but also as good business in its own right.

1 http://nin.tl/9VsA4U 2 http://nin.tl/aBiHi5 3 *Popular Mechanics*, 1 Oct 2009, http://nin.tl/9zw59i 4 Privacy Rights Clearinghouse http://nin.tl/clBooH 5 Chad Terhune, 'The Trouble With Background Checks', *Business Week*, 9 Jun 2008. 6 *The Register*, 30 Jan 2009, http://nin.tl/bis2of 7 http://nin.tl/aUFrFa 8 careerbuilder.com survey, 2009. 9 Reuters, 8 Sep 2009, http://nin.tl/9hjF7D 10 *Daily Telegraph*, 26 Feb 2009, http://nin.tl/cY467p 11 ZDNet UK, 9 Jan 2009, http://nin.tl/abL3yq 12 *Times Online*, 16 Jan 2008, http://nin.tl/9UildD 13 Richard J Bonnie, 'Political use of psychiatry in the Soviet Union and China: complexities and controversies', LLB, http://nin.tl/cGrZ62 14 http://nin.tl/dC7ipe 15 http://nin.tl/ciJ4zX 16 *National Law Journal*, 30 May 1994. 17 Simson Garfinkel, *Database Nation*, O'Reilly, 2000. 18 *New York Times*, 8 Aug 2009, http://nin.tl/coGZsN 19 ACLU, http://nin.tl/cmnwe8 20 *Washington Post*, 8 May 2009, http://nin.tl/daWYf9 21 *Daily Mail*, 12 Nov 2009 http://nin.tl/cVBvtB 22 *Birmingham Post*, 31 Aug 2009, http://nin.tl/cgbZXo 23 http://nin.tl/dvqs8S 24 BBC news, 23 Dec 2007, http://nin.tl/9akeFe 25 *Times Online*, 27 Sep 2009, http://nin.tl/cYkpeD 26 *Daily Telegraph*, 3 Mar 2009, http://nin.tl/aXVl4H 27 Frank J Donner, *The Age of Surveillance*, Alfred A Knopf, 1980. 28 wired.com 2 Oct 2008, http://nin.tl/ax5NQg 29 AFP, 26 Jan 2010, http://nin.tl/aNauLG 30 www.aclu.org/FilesPDFs/surveillance_report.pdf 31 See footnote 3. 32 *New York Times*, 14 Apr 2002, http://nin.tl/9L8Dwj 33 John Reid, 'Liberty, Resilience & Security in a Changing World', speech on 31 Oct 2006. 34 European Commission, http://ec.europa.eu/enterprise/security/index_en.htm 35 ECT News Network, 25 April 2005, http://nin.tl/aBw5AU 36 *The Independent*, 29 Jun 2008, http://nin.tl/aA3pVy 37 *Private Eye*, 8-21 Jan 2010.

7 The politics of fear

The threat of terrorism is being used as an excuse worldwide for surveillance and control measures that are undermining human rights. And individuals are complicit in this war on privacy by surrendering their own data for fun.

YOU CAN'T ENJOY freedom if you're dead. That is the mantra of the security industry, which is repeated by governments justifying their clampdowns on civil liberties and their invasions of privacy. In the face of ecological meltdown and an exploding global population – and having outsourced and delegated their power to private contractors – states can no longer promise to improve lives, but instead can only try to stop things getting worse and offer 'protection'. And that protection may require the kind of governance that wars used to be fought to prevent – where privacy and the presumption of innocence, as well as freedom from arbitrary arrest and torture, are all set aside.

It is true that people also have the right to live without fear of crime or terrorism, but they might need some persuading that the kind of draconian measures adopted in such a state could be justified in their name. Ironically, the most effective means of winning acquiescence for repressive laws and intensive surveillance is to terrorize people into acceptance, to create a global society in which anyone and everyone is to be feared and suspected, from new boyfriends through men in beards to almost any person on board an aircraft. Former Secretary of State Colin Powell admitted that terrorists could not destroy the US, that only the US could really do that. 'We shouldn't do it to ourselves, and we shouldn't use fear for political purposes – scaring people to death so they will vote for you, or scaring people to death so that we create a terror-industrial complex... creating an industry that will only exist as long as you keep the terrorist threat pumped up.'[1]

Former British Home Secretary John Reid made a similar observation: 'It would be easy to pump the politics of fear... But this is not the basis for advancing our values today. It is as undesirable an approach as it is a blunt instrument; the risks are too complex for that.' It was ironic that Reid went on, in the same speech, to claim that the UK was facing the severest threat since the Third Reich was bombing London and throttling the country's food supplies while invading the rest of the world.

A report by the International Commission of Jurists has concluded: 'Many governments, ignoring the lessons of history, have allowed themselves to be rushed into hasty responses to terrorism that have undermined cherished values and violated human rights.'[2] Among those cherished rights is *habeas corpus*, the requirement for those holding people in detention to explain their reasons for doing so in open court. This has been in place in England since the 12th-century Magna Carta, and has since been imported into the laws of many other countries. But it has effectively been torched in the past decade of legislation such as the Patriot Act in the US and the various anti-terror acts passed in Australia, Canada, New Zealand and the UK. These have seen Western countries copying not historic legal rights and freedoms but the kinds of practices more common in authoritarian 'allies' such as Pakistan and Saudi Arabia.

Between 2000 and 2008, the UK Parliament passed no fewer than six acts focusing on terrorism – leaving aside any further international treaties and agreements that were also entered into. The government played up the threats posed by crime and terrorism, claiming that security and crime were voters' top priorities. Law by law, the exceptional was used to justify the unacceptable and make it the norm.

The politics of fear

The Terrorism Act 2000 expanded the time allowed for terrorist suspects to be detained for questioning without charge to seven days. This was doubled to 14 days by the 2003 Criminal Justice Act, then doubled again under the 2006 Terrorism Act. Tony Blair's bid to increase this to 90 days – which would have put Britain on a par with apartheid-era South Africa – led to his first defeat in the House of Commons. A kind of apartheid in terms of justice for foreigners was, however, already in place. The post-9/11 Anti-terrorism, Crime and Security Act allowed for indefinite detention of foreigners as terrorist suspects. When the Law Lords struck this down as unconstitutional, a new act in 2005 created control orders that put suspects under house arrest (in breach of the European Convention on Human Rights). They had to surrender their passports, have their phones tapped, their friends needed official approval to visit, and they were required to report daily to a police station. The provision for secret evidence meant that suspects need not be told even the 'gist' of the case against them. In Australia, suspects could be preventatively detained without evidence of criminal involvement and be interrogated by the Australian Security Intelligence Organization, then gagged from telling anyone about this dirty little secret.

Such laws were passed on the big sell of non-existent threats. In January 2003, police rumbled a terrorist lair in Wood Green, London, where the deadly toxin ricin was allegedly being made. Tony Blair said this proved the terrorist danger was 'real and present', although lab tests later proved there was no ricin, and the defendants were acquitted of all counts (bar one, who had already been imprisoned for murder). But the 'ricin plot' passed into Home Office lore to justify new terror laws, to renew control order sunset clauses, to put orders on 10 further men linked to the plot while they were in jail (a Kafkaesque smear later admitted to as a 'mistake'). The Home Office was also mentioned in Colin Powell's February 2003 presentation to the UN Security Council about the (non-existent) threat of Iraq's (non-existent) WMD and al-Qaeda's (non-) involvement with Saddam Hussein. When the secret services will connive with democratically elected governments to wage war on lies, and get away with it, what hope is there for mere citizens?

Another non-event was the April 2004 raid by 400 police officers on a half dozen properties around Manchester, arresting eight men, a woman and a 16-year-old boy. After several days' interrogation, all were released without charge. But the story as it was leaked to the press was that police had foiled a suicide attack on the Old Trafford football ground: 'MAN U [Manchester United] SUICIDE BOMB PLOT' screamed the front page of *The Sun* newspaper. The basis for this nonsense was that one of the suspects, a Kurdish asylum seeker, had a poster of Old Trafford on his wall and had kept two ticket stumps as souvenirs from a game seen with a friend – this, it was claimed, was reconnaissance for an attack where they would sit apart so as to maximize casualties. This terrifying smear certainly ruined the suspects' lives, while the police made themselves look heroic, foiling a plot that never was.

Terror toys

Sometimes governments do not even bother to fabricate facts. This is when crude state terror toys like the Threat Condition Terror Alerts come into their own. These kiddy-color-coded levels go from LOW (green) up to SEVERE (red) and are issued regularly in ways that worry the public but don't burden them with such complexities as an underlying explanation or justification. These yo-yoing alerts – which never hit LOW – serve to keep the public pliable enough to accept whatever security measures the government throws at them.[3] How random the levels are is shown by the fact that UK levels were lowered just before the 7/7 attacks on public transport in London. More suspicious was the raising of the US threat level before the 2004 presidential elections in which Republicans charged the Democrat candidate John Kerry as being soft on terrorism. In January 2010 the UK Home Office, backed by MI5 and the Joint Terrorism Analysis Centre, raised the terror threat to 'severe', which Home Secretary Alan Johnson said was in response to the Underwear bomber a month before, though he admitted there was 'no intelligence' suggesting an imminent attack.[4]

Another alarming gimmick was Congress listing 160 sites as potentially important national targets for would-be terrorists. By 2007 this list contained an incredible 300,000 items, including an Illinois Apple and Pork Festival. In case you're nowhere near a Telescreen in the airport or mall imparting the latest terrifying non-event, websites such as www.national-terroralert.com can deliver all the intel you need about dirty bombs and suitcase nukes and what to do in case of attacks. Alternatively a live RSS feed of all the latest alert updates and terrifying news can be sent to your Facebook page or iPhone.

Dame Stella Rimington, MI5 chief from 1992 to 1996, accused UK ministers of 'frightening people' so as to pass laws interfering with people's privacy and civil liberties, achieving 'precisely one of the objects of terrorism: that we live in fear and under a police state.'[5] An example of this was when the UK government used its EU presidency to produce the report 'Liberty and Security: Striking the Right Balance'. This balanced document had a cover photo of the carnage caused by the 7/7 bombings and was effectively a manifesto demanding a raft of EU-wide surveillance measures. The International Commission of Jurists' report accused the US and

UK, among others, of 'actively undermining' the law through illegal counter-terrorism measures, creating a dangerous situation where terrorism, and the fear of terrorism, were undermining basic principles of international human rights law.

The European Court of Human Rights ruled in January 2010, for example, that the British police's stop and search powers under Section 44 of the 2000 Terrorism Act were too broad. Section 44 allows British police autonomously to designate 'areas' – even whole counties – where constables can stop and search anyone, without suspicion. In 2007-08, just 0.6 per cent of Section 44 stop and searches resulted in an arrest, but black and Asian people were up to seven times more likely to be fleeced, and Section 44's overwhelming use has been to harass anti-war protestors.[6] Section 44 is still awaiting amendment.[7] UK police interpret the 2008 Counter-Terrorism Act as allowing them to stop and search anyone taking a photo in public place. In 2009 Italian art student Simona Bonomo could not prove to the police that she was filming buildings in Paddington 'for fun', so she was arrested and locked up for five hours. Worse, she was given a fixed penalty fine for 'harassment, alarm and distress' – a 'downgraded' offense that no longer needs the approval of a court trial or allows the accused any due process.[8]

Meanwhile, in the name of the 'War on Terror', terrorist suspects are transported under the CIA's 'extraordinary rendition' program to outsourced torture centers in eastern Europe or the Middle East. Hundreds of such flights have been made over Europe with the knowledge and complicity of the EU's senior governments. Extraordinary rendition was started under the Clinton administration, and expanded wholesale under the George W Bush administration. It was based on the medieval idea that torture is necessary and effective – as opposed to a technique that leads people to confess to anything that will make the pain stop. A traumatized US public saw this view brought into the 21st century in the TV series *24*, in which the ends of averting terrorist atrocities regularly and repeatedly justify any means, including torture.[9]

Canadian citizen Maher Ahar ended up facing a year of torture in Axis of Evil acolyte Syria under the extraordinary rendition program. His 'crime' was vaguely knowing the brother of a colleague under Canadian surveillance. This got Ahar onto a US terrorist list, at which point, with Canadian intelligence co-operation, he was arrested, interrogated and flown to Syria. He was ultimately released, exonerated, and the Canadian government was forced to apologize. Still, Canadian intelligence would later see Ahar's brother-in-law picked up and questioned by security forces in Tunisia.[10]

The infamous US Camp X-Ray in Guantánamo Bay, Cuba, is still open despite President Obama's promise to close it. This is because the Department of Justice advised that 47 of its 192 inmates should be held indefinitely, as they were too dangerous to release but there was insufficient concrete evidence to convince a court.[11] This is despite the view of the International Commission of Jurists that Guantánamo torture, like the Iraq War itself, would only create more suicide terrorists with 'greater justification'. Detention without charge has also been extended to US citizens under the 2006 Military Commissions Act, which codified what the Patriot Act originally intended.

A top UK Foreign Office advisor warned Tony Blair in 2004 that British foreign policy in the Middle East was a 'recurring theme' in creating 'anger and impotence' among young male Muslims in the UK, a warning supported by think-tank Chatham House and later by former MI5 chief Eliza Manningham Butler. Security expert Crispin Black asserted that

Blair was so averse to the idea of blowback that, prior to 7/7, intelligence services were directed away from investigating and pre-empting such a line of attack – again, intelligence was directed to fit policy, but the natural consequence of 7/7 was that there were yet more security measures.

According to former US National Security Advisor Zbigniew Brzezinski: 'Fear obscures reason, intensifies emotions and makes it easier for demagogic politicians to mobilize the public on behalf of the policies they want to pursue,'[12] under the aegis of the vague umbrella phrase 'War on Terror'. When there are no terrorist attacks, it does not prove the absence of threat, but rather that governments' counter-terrorism strategies are working. Any further attack, however, proves the need for yet more security measures.

Targeting children

Repressive anti-terror measures are often enacted in the name of protecting people, including children. Yet children are caught up in the web of suspicion. In 2008, 386 under-18s had their DNA taken and stored by British police in Camden, north London, as part of a 'long-term' crime prevention strategy. The police theory was that anyone knowing their DNA was on the database would 'think twice' before becoming a professional criminal, an attitude that civil liberties groups said showed a 'diabolical' contempt for children's freedom. However, Scotland Yard's director of forensic sciences and the Association of Chief Police Officers' DNA spokesperson Gary Pugh argued it was necessary to find who was 'possibly going to be the biggest threat to society'. The reasoning was that children usually start offending between 10 and 13 years old but that risk factors for 'likely' offenders could be identified in children as young as 5 to 7 years old. The Public Policy Research Institute's report *Make Me a Criminal* called for cognitive behavioral therapy, parenting programs and intensive support to be directed at children between the ages of 5 and 12 – although the report's author conceded this could, as the National Primary Headteachers' Association warned, condemn children at a very young age for 'something they have not yet done', and stigmatize children for life.[13]

The ONSET database, meanwhile, profiles children suspected of being bullied, living in poor housing or a low-income family, or any other factors that predispose children to criminality. The online Common Assessment Framework (eCAF) that gauges if children need extra state inputs in health or education, collects subjective data on 'dubious legal grounds' to pre-empt problems like teenage pregnancies or criminality, although evidence to support this approach is almost non-existent.[14]

Children can be asked to participate in the monitoring. Students aged 12 at British school Birkdale High in 2009 were tasked with picking out five boys who might do well or might disrupt lessons so that they could be listed on the school's 'behavior database'.[15] US teachers can deliver grade-oriented lessons on the wonderful world of spying by basing them on the FBI and CIA children's web pages (www.fbi.gov/fbikids, www.cia.gov/kids-page), in which kids learn about surveillance through play. One in six UK councils employs young children as Junior Streetwatchers (8-10 year olds) or Street Scene Champions (11-14 year olds), in which they are given James Bond-style numbers for their espionage work reporting dog fouling or failed recycling efforts. With large cash rewards for evidence leading to a conviction, children learn to equate citizenship with spying and monetary reward.[16]

In this sense, we should perhaps fear the clean, morally upright child as much as the feral youths we seek to pre-empt. However, we are also encouraged to fear for all children. As with the CCTV craze after the murder of Jamie Bulger in 1993 (see page 84), certain child murders in the UK have become *causes célèbres* that have helped validate and bring surveillance schemes into being. The plight of eight-year-old Victoria Climbie, who died in 2000 after years of abuse at the hands of her guardians, was so well known to police, doctors and social services, that after her death investigations marked a dozen points where services could have intervened and saved her – but for systematic failures in following procedures by overworked and badly led social workers. But Climbie's sad case was used to sell the solution of ContactPoint, a £224-million ($340-million) database that could be accessed by 390,000 public-service workers. It was to be built to hold an unprecedented amount of data about every child in the UK, whether they were at risk or not, before it was scrapped as a result of the change of British government in 2010.

Similarly, the Safeguarding Vulnerable Groups Act 2006 was fired by the murders of two 10-year-old girls, Holly Wells and Jessica Chapman, by the caretaker of their school. The caretaker had been given the job despite having previously been investigated in connection with sexual offenses and burglary, because police forces bungled the vetting procedures. The Act created in response set up the Vetting and Barring Scheme to regulate 'instances where a relationship of trust might develop between a 'vulnerable person' and another individual.[17] This initially meant, for example, that plumbers would need vetting because they visit homes and children live in homes. It was planned that a sixth of the UK population, some 11.3 million people 'working with children', were to be put on the database before the guidelines were relaxed.

The hassle and cost of such checks has dissuaded innocent and otherwise enthusiastic adults from running children's activities, such as sports clubs, has left hundreds of thousands without work or income for up to eight weeks, and blighted the lives of adults with minor criminal convictions which have nothing to do with sex crimes or offenses against children. Celebrities giving talks at schools must pay £64 ($100) to prove they're not a pedophile – although MPs are exempt.

Such measures to protect children and vulnerable adults ultimately destroy the fabric of the society that is trying to keep them safe. One woman had not been vetted and so could not kiss her daughter goodbye on a school trip;[18] another mother was told she needed a Criminal Records Bureau check to continue taking her severely epileptic son to school by taxi; while in 2009 Manor Community College in Cambridge banned anyone from its premises who had not been officially vetted as child safe.[19]

The 1994 Sexual Offender Act in the US allowed details of convicted sex offenders to be divulged to their local communities, the Act being dubbed 'Megan's Law' in honor of the child whose murder inspired it. Research indicated that Megan's Law did not impact on offender recidivism, nor on the severity of such crimes, nor did it prevent first-time offenses. Nevertheless, the murder of Sarah Payne in 2000 by a convicted pedophile led to British calls for a similar 'Sarah's Law'. A one-year pilot scheme in four local authorities led to the announcement in August 2010 that the scheme would be rolled out nationally.

In 2008, numerous English police forces allowed parents and guardians to check out anyone with access to their child – as with single mothers wanting to find out about their new boyfriend. This scheme, like others, NSPCC policy chief Diana Sutton says, delivers both a 'false sense of security' and a false sense of danger: 'We only know who the convicted pedophiles are – what about the rest of humanity?' The logic has become so twisted that Telford and Wrekin Council decided police and park wardens could approach anyone walking alone in the park on suspicion that they could be looking for children.[20]

Most sex offenders are never caught, for most offenses occur within the family, but whether or not there are actually any more predators than there were in the good old days, what matters is the perception that there are. 'Stranger danger' has led to more children being driven to school and added to accident rates involving children and cars, statistically a far greater danger to children than abduction.[21]

The concept of 'risk' to children is a global one. British Airways, Qantas and Air New Zealand have long insisted that men cannot sit next to children unknown to them on flights. The head of Interpol's fingerprint unit, Mark Branchflower, told the Biometrics 2008 conference that immigration control points needed enhanced fingerprint and automatic facial recognition technology to catch anyone that Interpol had filed as a threat – regardless of how that assessment came to pass in the first place.[22] At a Russian conference on internet rights in 1999, Austrian campaigner Erich Moechel released official summary documents from international police working groups showing that the authorities clearly intended to exploit public concern about child pornography as a 'strategy' to promote efforts to place the internet under surveillance.[23]

Keeping children safely locked up indoors often exposes them, of course, to the internet and its own universe of dangers and predators. Software company Spectorsoft offers SpectorPro for monitoring all computer and internet usage on home and office PCs, so you can be Big Boss or Big Mother, recording chats, instant messages, emails, websites, keystrokes, including MySpace and Facebook activity recording – 'so you will know everything your kids are posting about themselves and everything your friends are posting about them'. Or, if you're not at home, use your laptop to spy on the children and the nanny directly with internal CCTV or with the 'nanny cams' offered by companies like www.my-spycam.com. In the face of all this, what hope is there for the concept of privacy?

The war on privacy

As Josef Goebbels once said: 'The only individual with a private life in Germany is the person who is asleep'... or as the Sun MicroSystems CEO Scott McNealy claimed: 'Privacy is dead, deal with it.'[24]

Historically, laws were written to preserve the balance of power between governments and citizens and to prevent unwarranted searches or abuse of state power. Privacy itself, though, was a more ethereal concept, an 'unenumerated', 'unspecified' or 'implicit' right as judged by courts.[25]

Technology made this a more pressing matter. In 1890, the *Harvard Law Review*'s article 'The Right to Privacy' cited Judge Cooley's definition of privacy as the right 'to be let alone' and be spared the 'great mental pain and distress' being wrought by new 'mechanical devices' of telephones, telegrams and instant photography to enable 'what is whispered in the closet [to] be proclaimed from the house-tops'. Photographic images circulated without permission backed up the industrialized gossip produced by unethical newspapers profiting from a stifling world of lies: 'No enthusiasm can flourish, no generous impulse can survive under its blighting influence.'[26]

Today's truly globalized industry is the processing, exchange and trade of innumerable factoids of personal data across thousands of databases worldwide for anyone to peruse for profit and power. Now, more than ever, as researcher Katherine Hayles writes: 'The rights to data protection and privacy are essential conditions in a democratic society to safeguard the respect for the rights of individuals, a free flow of information and an open market economy... Without privacy, the coercive force of hegemonic power to control not only behavior but the innermost thoughts of citizens becomes absolute.'[27]

The right to privacy is not just an abstract, but is central to democracy and the balance of rights between the state and the individual. Soviet states sought to stifle any individual self-expression deemed at odds with the Party's mold of human, curtailing also their freedom of movement, political thought and religion.[28] The Party arrogated to itself the right to get into citizens' heads by fear, with every citizen aware of a file somewhere on them and their lack of control over that file's contents. As Maria Los writes: 'Assumed but almost never encountered, the file was envisaged as a secret, central paper folder, somewhere in the Ministry of the Interior, where all the undesirable information about us would inevitably end up... The belief that everybody had a secret file was far from accurate, but [this] assumption was essential to the underlying total control strategy.'[29]

Privacy in a totalitarian state was one thing, but, as the Eastern Bloc and Soviet Union imploded between 1989 and 1991, concerns about privacy violations in the 'free' West were mounting. The 1990 Calcutt Committee on Privacy and Related Matters was reasserting individuals' rights to privacy as the right to their or their families' personal life and affairs being protected against intrusion 'by direct physical means or by publication of information'. People had to be empowered to control the information about them and who could access it, with strong boundaries set down between the private and public spheres and respected by everyone from the president to the till-worker.

But globalization demands no boundaries – a 'borderless world', as noted by the 30th International Conference of Data Protection and Privacy Commissioners in 2009. The Conference – along with countless other international bodies – considers that there is still the 'urgent need' to protect privacy, and called for 'the universal character' of rights to data protection and privacy to be protected under a universal convention, 'appealing' to the UN to prepare a legally binding instrument making such rights fundamental and enforceable.

Treaties and laws protecting privacy already exist, the concept writ global by the UN Declaration of Human Rights, which, under Article 17, provided for each person to be protected 'against arbitrary or unlawful interference with his privacy, family, home or correspondence as well as against unlawful attacks on his honor and reputation.' Article 8 of the European Convention on Human Rights (ECHR) contains a very similar clause. The 1998 UK Data Protection Act requires that organizations holding data about individuals must retain it only for as long as necessary, with adequate security, must use it only for specific purposes, not for marketing, and must cause neither damage nor distress. The Fourth Amendment of the US Bill of Rights, states that 'people have the right to be secure in their persons, houses, papers, and effects, against unreasonable searches and seizures, shall not be violated, and no Warrants shall issue, but upon probable cause...'. Even the USSR's 1977 constitution provided for the inviolability of the person and home, and the right to privacy.

Yet all these provisions may be rendered worthless because the state and its partners always demand exceptions. The ECHR Article 8 demands 'no interference by a public authority with the exercise of this right', unless 'such as is in accordance with the law and is necessary in a democratic society in the interests of national security, public safety or the economic well-being of the country, for the prevention of disorder or crime, for the protection of health or morals, or for the protection of the rights and freedoms of others.' This is such a broad range of justifications that it in practice allows the state to invade any citizen's privacy.

There will always be such exceptions. Under the US's 1978 Foreign Intelligence Surveillance Act, the Department of Justice set up a court to handle government requests for warrants for covert eavesdropping, and from 1979 to 2000, they had over 13,000 applications – of which just two were modified, and five refused. There was still at least the semblance of a 'signature prohibition' on domestic covert wiretapping of civilians, but 9/11 brought that to an end.

Then there is the domestic use of ECHELON.[30] Those involved in the program have told Congress there are no formal controls as to who can be targeted, ranging from dangerous radicals such as Martin Luther King, John Lennon and Jane Fonda, to the wiretapping of staunchly patriotic, Republican Senator Strom Thurmond during the late 1980s. After the death of Princess Diana the NSA admitted it had 1,056 pages of classified information on her, without revealing its sources.[31] In 1999, Congress member Bob Barr sought Congressional investigation of ECHELON, accusing the NSA of carrying out a 'dragnet' of communications and 'invading the privacy of American citizens'.[32] But 9/11 has only meant that eavesdropping facilities once aimed at the outside world have turned inwards.[33]

Doublethink and the need for a room of our own

While many have sought to protect privacy, those seeking to demolish it have worked with increasing vigor. In Western countries, the meme of 'nothing to hide, nothing to fear' has proved very effective in the push for ever more 'security'. When concepts like privacy or freedom of speech are up for 'discussion', one senses that governments will give the advocates of privacy half a euro to phone someone who cares.

Thus, for example, in 2007, the UK Treasury

made public its aim to shift the law's position regarding data-sharing from requiring individuals' consent to one of default sharing. This 'over-arching vision' of data-sharing having been in place since the 1990s, Privacy International's only surprise was that the British government had taken so long, yet still 'with such disregard for even the most basic safe-guards.'[34] Clause 152 of the innocuous-sounding 2009 Coroners' and Justice Act enabled the 'extraordinarily broad' sharing of information by ministerial order and allowed any person to be empowered to share information, including personal data, with others for purposes other than those for which it was originally obtained. As Privacy International noted, this would allow, among a phonebook of terrors, NHS files to be used for medical research and insurance without patient consent; private and corporate investigators to access police intelligence; and for personal financial data to be shared between government departments and with intelligence and security services, without parliamentary approval. If nothing else, there is the malevolence of ineptitude. In 2009 the Rowntree Trust found that 11 out of 46 public-sector databases in the UK clearly breached European data protection and rights laws.[35] Meanwhile, those Stasi files shred-ded by panicking East German agents in 1989 are being painstakingly reconstructed, allowing for the lives of others to be trawled through again. The files of Romania's Securitate are still largely intact.[36]

Admiral Poindexter remarked of Total Information Awareness that it would create 'technologies that would permit us have both security and privacy'. The Asia-Pacific Economic Community's 2004 Privacy Framework said something similar, bidding to 'strengthen privacy protection and maintain informa-tion flows' – but it's all doublethink, a contradiction in terms. Information is profit as well as power, people having become partly inured to governments' mass dissemination and retention of their data because banks and supermarkets do it already. Facebook, Twitter and Google are as complicit as states in their assaults on privacy and their orchestration of surveillance – they make online exhibitionism 'fun' while retaining the data forever for the world to trawl and gawp at.[37] It enables the press to data-mine as they conflate 'the public interest' and 'what interests the public' with their own salacious purposes, substituting titbits found on Facebook for investigative journalism. It also flies in the face of the French concept of the 'right to be forgotten' (*Droit à l'Oubli*), to be able to walk away from some awkward facts of one's life.[38]

It could, of course, be said that the users of sites like Facebook are responsible for whatever information they upload, that they are to blame if they don't read the terms of agreement which specify that user content can be mined and sold to third parties if not given up according to a host-state's law. They should not fool themselves that all these sites host their content for free. But companies adjust and rewrite their terms and conditions. Facebook changed its terms and conditions without warning in 2009 in order to retain and own all data forever for any purpose it saw fit. Users were told they could remove content any time, but 'the Company may retain archived copies of your User Content'.[39] The ensuing uproar led to Facebook changing tack and inviting users to 'adjust' their privacy settings from a new default which allowed their data to be left open for anyone to find on the internet. According to the Electronic Frontier Foundation, this was a move 'clearly intended' to push Facebook users to publicly share even more information than before and reduce user control over data.[40]

Facebook has lobbying teams in Washington and Brussels dedicated to making governments 'understand our philosophy' on internet privacy and data sharing and helping 'well-meaning' legislators' understand that their efforts to protect consumers may keep people 'from the beneficial sharing of information'. The Open Rights Group noted the ease with which businesses lobby Brussels and shape vital legislation in ways that concerned citizens could not match.[41] Not least when companies like Google have as their founding mission 'to organize the world's information and make it universally accessible and useful' – but for what and for whom?

The Big Brother aspect of the internet is having a chilling effect on people. The internet is becoming less about protecting and serving the public than about power protecting itself. The discovery of an unregulated, private space is a central theme in Orwell's *Nineteen Eighty-Four*. Spaces where 'unauthorized, rebellious, and even dangerous thoughts can be entertained; they are also catalysts to discovery, innovation, and potential change'. This makes privacy a 'positive social good' that fosters the creativity, innovation and maybe even the rebellion and deviancy essential for society's renewal. In Doris Lessing's 1978 short story *To Room Nineteen*, the heroine's private room is her sanctum for creativity, but it creates suspicions in her husband's mind and he sends a private investigator after her. Her privacy violated, she abandons the room and her creativity is destroyed.

But threats to creativity, the stifling of innovation, the invitation to self-censorship: these are difficult arguments to present to the public in a way that truly resonates. It comes back to the mantra 'you can't enjoy freedom when you're dead'. How important are nice books, people say, in the face of being blown up?[42]

According to surveillance expert Maria Los: 'As people accumulate illuminating personal experiences of unforeseen effects of surveillance on their life, they will gradually recognize that surveillance is not an abstract feature of environment or culture but has tangible personal consequences that need to be reckoned with'.[43] Or, put another way, by international security expert Patrick Radden Keefe: 'The public is suffering "boiling frog" syndrome, until some future point whereupon "we find ourselves wondering how we got here"'.[44] People have little issue with wholesale general surveillance, but if they are asked 'should the government be able to sift through what DVDs you watch or what books you read?', they will see that as problematic. But by that point it may be too late.

1 *GQ* 12 Sep 2007. 2 *Daily Telegraph*, 16 Feb 2009 http://nin.tl/axgnKX 3 http://terror-alert.uscg.org/ 4 BBC news, Jan 2010, http://nin.tl/d2wYnh 5 See footnote 2. 6 Liberty, Jul 2003, http://nin.tl/9XsbKK 7 Liberty, 12 Jan 2010, http://nin.tl/c3MTVr & http://nin.tl/9bs4mA 8 *The Guardian*, 15 Dec 2009, http://nin.tl/agG9rt 9 ACLU, http://nin.tl/bYjRaK 10 http://www.i-cams.org/ICAMS1.pdf 11 BBC news, 22 Jan 2010, http://nin.tl/9xZwkt 12 Zbigniew Brzezinski, 'Terrorized by the war on terror', *Washington Post*, 25 Mar 2007. 13 *The Observer*, 16 Mar 2008, http://nin.tl/aLHAOw 14 Joseph Rowntree Reform Trust, http://nin.tl/d2bfdG 15 http://nin.tl/dyZNWZ 16 *Daily Telegraph*, 5 Sep 2008, http://nin.tl/dytRpf 17 *The Independent*, 18 Jul 2009, http://nin.tl/9yP8rT 18 *Daily Telegraph*, 10 July 2008, http://nin.tl/aEApTp 19 *Metro*, 8 Dec 2009. 20 'On your own in the park... are you a pervert?' *Metro*, 10 Sep 2008. 21 BBC news, 8 Dec 2009, http://nin.tl/daDKlR 22 *The Guardian*, 20 Oct 2008, http://nin.tl/cAV92l 23 Simon Davies, 'Privacy Matters', *Index on Censorship*, 3/00. 24 MSNBC, 8 Dec 2000, http://nin.tl/aN8J1S 25 Liberty, *Overlooked*, 2007. 26 Samuel D Warren and Louis D Brandeis, 'The Right to Privacy', *Harvard Law Review* 15 Dec 1890, http://nin.tl/9NNo9G 27 N Katherine Hayles, *Waking Up to the Surveillance Society*, Duke University, 2009. 28 Henry Porter, http://nin.tl/agoKjs 29 Maria Los, in David Lyon (ed), *Theorizing Surveillance - the panopticon and beyond*, Willan Publishing, 2006. 30 Duncan Campbell, *New Statesman*, 12 Aug 1988, http://nin.tl/9eRbVb 31 *Washington Post*, 12 Dec 1998, http://nin.tl/9qM5mi 32 BBC news, 3 Nov 1999, http://nin.tl/a4Ksrn 33 Patrick Radden Keefe, Statewatch seminar, London, May 2009. 34 Privacy International, http://nin.tl/culB4a 35 *The Guardian*, 23 Mar 2009, http://nin.tl/axjjWs 36 BBC news, 10 Dec 2009, http://nin.tl/bYGlWg 37 Dr Kieron O'Hara, University of Southampton, *Evening Standard*, 7 Jan 2010. 38 www.peterfleischer.blogspot.com 39 Chris Walters, *The Consumerist*, 15 Feb 2009, http://nin.tl/a4B4wC 40 BBC news, 10 Dec 2009 http://nin.tl/cGfP4h 41 *The Guardian*, 26 Jun 2009, http://nin.tl/9fZ659 42 Larry Siems, Statewatch seminar, May 2009. 43 See footnote 29. 44 See footnote 33.

8 Brave new world

Surveillance systems have a life of their own – they creep into new areas, absorb more powers. The danger is that we are creating a world built on distrust in which there will be literally no escape from those who are watching us.

COMPUTERS, ALGORITHMS AND databases are designed by people, maintained by people, programmed and uploaded by people, yet are somehow considered infallible, whatever use they are put to. The phenomenon of 'function creep' means there is a perennial tendency to redeploy a device or method used in one area to any number of additional uses – way beyond what was originally envisaged, or consented to. Britons were issued with ID cards during World War Two to distinguish them from German spies. By the time of their abolition in 1952, the cards were linked to some 40 daily functions. Function creep allows the maximum political and financial return to be made on the investment, whether through rescuing a bad decision by finding a better use for some gizmo, or through 'revolutionizing' a system. Decades later, the logic repeats itself and a system like the National Identity Register, ostensibly built to keep the Britons' data secure, can be better funded by selling the data held on it.

Every new database is built in the name of security and protection, but every database is hackable. Microsoft's Jerry Fishenden warned that the National Identity Register could become a 'honeypot' for theft, with the inherent risk of 'massive identity fraud on a scale beyond anything we have seen before'.[1] Such systems require the most up-to-date, secure software, yet every new IT system suffers months of glitches and vulnerabilities, 'teething troubles' requiring a blizzard of patches, and these are clearly unacceptable when a nation's data is at stake. Security depends on the least number of people being authorized to access databases on a strict need-to-know basis, but these databases are being built for access by entire governments and private-sector partners, possibly millions of people of whom 'some will be wicked, and many more will be careless'.[2]

There is no database (or RFID, or biometric) that cannot be hacked, and people and computers combined can make excellent disasters of increasing scale. In October 2007, two discs containing the entire child-benefit database of 25 million Britons were lost. Two months later, the details of three million US driving-test candidates were lost, the same month that nine UK NHS trusts admitted losing the details of hundreds of thousands of patients.

If you can't catch criminals, you criminalize those you can catch. FBI agents have uploaded many onto No Fly Lists who are guilty of no more than subscribing to 'subversive' publications such as anti-war magazines – some have fallen victim to this because agents have to meet a certain quota of uploads per week. This all contributes to the quashing of dissent, and meshes with the increasingly sophisticated targeting of voters by political marketing teams, creating a vice of control that crushes genuine democracy. Concerns about police intimidation and privacy mean a third of Britons are disinclined to participate in protests,[3] while every ironic comment made on Facebook, on a blog, in an email, text or tweet, every photo, every page visited, is retained forever for sifting.

CCTV footage sold to worldwide tabloid TV franchises like *The World's Wildest Police Videos* serves to terrify the public into believing the world outside is a non-stop riot requiring constant police and CCTV presence. Some idiots create incidents for these few seconds of infamy. At its worst extreme this has involved youths using mobile phone cameras to record 'happy slapping' (assaulting someone, usually a stranger), gang rape, or even, in the London district of Waterloo one night, a murder, and then distribute the film to their friends or across the internet. New technology allows for new crimes. In 2006, two CCTV operatives for Sefton Council in Liverpool were jailed for spying on a naked woman in her home. In 2009 the Met closed down 20 ID card factories in London, part of a £14-million ($21-million) racket.[4] Identity fraud is a growing problem – as evidenced by the Israeli security service Mossad cloning a dozen passports of British citizens to enable a team to carry out the assassination of Hamas leader Mahmoud al-Mabhou in January 2010.[5]

Databases and the data held on them are only as good or secure as the people that build, fill, file and maintain them – and they are often ill-trained, under-paid, unmotivated and overworked. Information is given out to people who sound convincing, offer bribes or make enough threats – the British Information Commissioner's office has found that private investigators can access the Criminal Records Bureau for only £500 ($750), a pittance for organized criminals, kidnappers or people traffickers.

Building bigger haystacks only makes finding needles more difficult. Scant resources are spent pursuing low-level concerns and false positives while the Underwear bomber is missed amid half a million other 'suspects'. As Steve Lukasik, former DARPA chief and terrorist-tracking team leader on Total Information Awareness, said, the system creates a 'screamingly large amount of false positives... None of this makes any sense if you find more innocent people than you find terrorists.'[6]

Attempts to create more secure governance in the face of danger tend to end up demolishing privacy and undermining democracy, actually creating greater dangers than those it was set up to counter. Estonia has often been held up as a paragon of how e-government can and should work, with citizens happily paying tax, voting and changing their registration details online. That was until spring 2007, when a 'distributed denial of service' brought government, commercial and bank websites grinding to a halt. Cabinet ministers could not access emails for four days, the main bank, Hannabank, suffered $1 million in losses. The attacks were small-scale, launched by a group of patriotic Russian hackers (or so Moscow claimed) in a row over a Second World War Soviet soldier statue in Tallinn. But it showed that an entire government could be derailed by a keyboard anywhere in the world.

Standardization also means that one vulnerability can compromise a global system. Some 80 per cent of the world's cellphones – four billion and counting – run on the Global System for Mobile Communication. This system purports to keep conversations and texts secure by the A5/1 algorithm that creates trillions of mathematical possibilities and makes it virtually unhackable. Yet a dedicated team of German scientists cracked the system with just $30,000 worth of kit.[7] Besides, for just $69.96, you can buy E-Stealth's Ultimate Mobile Phone Spy to hack Bluetooth-enabled mobiles and laptops and stop your partner 'cheating on you and making secret calls in the bathroom' (buy now, says E-Stealth, before the US Department of Justice takes it off the market[8]).

Armed with no more than a wired-up PC and a 'how to hack' book, self-confessed British nerd Gary McKinnon repeatedly hacked into the networks of the Pentagon and NASA in his quest to find out about UFOs. He was caught in 2009 and is at the time of publication still fighting extradition to the US, where he could face a 40-year jail sentence. It was exactly this kind of vulnerability that prevented the UK's security services from digitizing their operations for many years.[9] US-based company MetroMail, now part of Experian, used prisoners for data-input tasks of customer surveys, with the possibly inevitable result that a convicted rapist and burglar started stalking grandmother Beverly Dennis with letters that cited her favourite soap and magazines. Whether he mentioned her hemorrhoid medicine, also in her 25-page dossier, was not disclosed at the trial in which she sued MetroMail.[10]

Supermarket sweep

An economy based on credit and debt demands increased discipline and surveillance. The normalization of wholesale surveillance began with the shopping malls that sprang up across the West in the 1980s. These controlled, sterile, commercial environments were built to sell goods to consumers heavily profiled by marketing databases, using credit cards cleared of risk by bank databases. Their behavior in the mall is directed by spatial design and monitored by CCTV systems that were initially human-operated but are now run by programs such as PointGrey's Censys3D People Tracking System, which has the dual purposes of security and consumer profiling.[11]

Public spaces have also come under the auspices of private surveillance, with individuals' privacy considered secondary to security considerations, while private homes and communications are also subject to increasing state and privately operated means of surveillance, in the name of consumer convenience and security.

Supermarkets have also been central to normalizing ID-card use. In the UK, 18 is the minimum age for alcohol, but shops demand ID for anyone who looks under 21, and shop staff have lately been urged to 'think 25'.[12] Hence, while the UK's ID card scheme may have been scrapped, having an ID card at all times is becoming a *de facto* requirement of the private sector. By late 2009 public support for ID cards had waned to the point where 60 per cent of Britons were unwilling to volunteer for a card,[13] so the private sector gamely stepped in to help make people 'accept that this is not only a necessary but desirable part of modern society over the next 10 years' as they become 'absolutely commonplace in the private sphere.'[14]

Shoppers surrender massive amounts of data to supermarkets for 'loyalty' cards, entitling the loyal to discounts on some goods, which may be subsidized by raising the prices of other goods, to the detriment of those too poor to warrant loyalty cards. (In Orwell's *Nineteen Eighty-Four* the proles cheered the news of an increased chocolate ration to 30gm, forgetting that it had only been cut to 20gm the day before.) Indeed, 75 per cent of supermarkets' profits come from just 30 per cent of their customers, and if that means clearing the shelves of rice to sell caviar, so be it.[15]

Social inequalities based on income become compounded and exacerbated by such profiling of customers, particularly if the supermarket has a monopoly in the area, which most do. Global firms like Tesco and Wal-Mart have expanded beyond groceries into all areas of life, including insurance, internet provision and estate agency, and are so pivotal in public works that they have a major influence on town planning decisions. RFIDs in goods produced, consumed and disposed of worldwide leave a global trail that links the purchaser and consumer to whatever environmental pollution or criminal enterprise they might end up in.

'Cradle-to-grave' applies to private corporations as much as to any over-arching state. At one end, there was the case of the woman who bought a pregnancy test kit on her credit card, only to find that, nine months later, she was being sent product information about diapers and baby milk. At the other end, Wal-Mart is selling coffins – from a 'Mom' or 'Dad

Remembered' steel coffin for $895 to a bronze model at $2,899,[16] while the profiles of deceased Facebook users can be memorialized on request.[17]

Superstores have also pushed for the privatization of police. ShopWatch is a program operated by London department stores which sponsor the training and deployment of voluntary special constables with powers of arrest and able to use handcuffs and weaponry (the idea has since been extended to HospitalWatch, BusBeat and CampusWatch[18]). In 2009, it was proposed that shopping malls should have their own detention centers in which offenders could be fingerprinted, photographed and DNA-sampled for up to four hours before their arrest.

Whereupon the fear is less the superstate running the place like a supermarket, with segregation and individualized targeting entrenching social divisions, but the supermarket becoming the state. How long before the trucks making home deliveries of comestibles instead disgorge security officers pre-emptively arresting any plebs who might commit shoplifting?

We should perhaps be concerned that the world is heading inexorably towards a system resembling China's 'Market Stalinism'. Chinese citizens are free in so far as they conform and consume to the benefit of the country's vast corporations, which in turn support the state in its repression of dissent. Such repression has been enabled by the Golden Shield, the world's largest domestic, single-database surveillance enterprise. The Ministry of Public Security conceived the Shield in 1998 to counter the threat posed by the China Democratic Party by having its members locked up. It has since been developed to combine surveillance and censorship and shield the state and its corporate supporters from disaffected people seeking a freer, democratic society.[19] The Great Firewall monitors and controls all internet access, with any dubious online activity or comments traced to source and arrests pursuant, intermittently abetted by Microsoft, Google and Yahoo! The plan is to create a 'gigantic online database with an all-encompassing surveillance network – incorporating speech and face recognition, closed-circuit television, smart cards, credit records, and internet surveillance technologies', according to the International Center for Human Rights and Democratic Development.[20]

Next door to China is North Korea, the Big Brother's Big Brother – starving, diplomatically isolated, economically throttled, poverty-stricken, its citizens bade to praise its ruling party and Great Leader while distrusting one another and all foreigners. North Korea lacks the technology and regular electricity supplies for CCTV and IT, supermarkets and banks; instead, the state's chief concern is individual's *songbun*, their place in society, which derives from their level of loyalty to the Revolution. Just as marketing firms stratify consumer societies, songbun is used to stratify North Korean society into three main classes and 51 sub-grades, with individuals' songbun graded by their own achievements or transgressions and those of their forebears – descendants of Korean revolutionaries and decorated combatants against the Japanese and the US have better prospects than the descendants of landowners and counter-revolutionaries. One person's crimes imprison their family, then and thereafter, with citizens' cards marked before they're born. North Korea is an extremely static society but the pariah state has survived through six decades that have included total war, sanctions, famine and ecological meltdown. The strongest surveillance can guarantee the state and its top guns can see out the worst disasters, regardless of the cost to civilians.

A more plausible model for Western countries might be the 20th-century Italian dictator Mussolini's corporate fascism, with businesses prospering under the 'enabling' state, which guarantees the security of its citizens.[21] Surveillance may currently be operating in the service of consumerism, but as the pressures of climate change, terrorism and population growth reduce the prosperity of richer, consuming nations this may change. The surveillance-security industry may then profit more from managing the national decline, enabling the state to protect itself from the disaffected, and fortifying them against the tides of refugees and asylum-seekers washing against their shores.

Grand plans and smart dust

The plans keep changing but the outcome is the same. The US's Total Information Awareness, Britain's ID cards and ContactPoint, have all been scrapped. But for every scrapped database or initiative there are hundreds more databases, public, private and combined, whirling away, yet mostly unknown. Across the US and Europe, scores of 'fusion centers' pool and sift all data, providing users, public and private, with a 'kaleidoscopic vision' of possible terrorist threats.[22] A prime example of the private-state security cross-over is Google, the world's most awesome private-sector retainer of personal data, negotiating with the US National Security Agency, which itself is said to harvest three Library of Congress' worth of data per day, to find 'vulnerabilities' with Google's operating systems.[23] Although one suspects that the NSA has all of Google's data already.

What could soon join up the RFIDs and GPS already embedded in cellphones phones, ID and credit-cards is a Real World Web of 'smart dust' sensors, a global web of trillions of tiny sensors deployed to monitor and transmit all data via Wi-Fi about cities, traffic, weather, the natural environment and people, like 'electronic nerve endings for the planet'.[24] Although this has been delayed by costs and technological holdups, firms are working on making cellphones into linked-up sensors that make people integral to the web that tracks them, ultimately creating what the Electronic Frontier Foundation called 'a very, very, very huge potential privacy invasion' by a vast, dynamic and near-undetectable global network.

Globalization is moving security away from guns and bombs to the environment and finance, from ideology to ethnicity, and where the US was once the dominant proponent of Cold War doctrines, now the EU, Canada, Japan and Australasia are part of the transnational security apparatus that views all Muslims as potential enemies. All citizens of the Global South must be databased and assessed for both their worth and their potential threat. Non-EU students coming to the UK must, for example, undergo points ratings, carry biometric ID and pay exorbitantly more in tuition fees, and yet are first in line for suspicion by university staff bidden to monitor Muslim and 'Asian-looking' students, and report anything dodgy to the Home Office or Special Branch, on pain of prison or fines for non-compliance.[25] This tsunami of data is being used to make decisions that we might once have been able to appeal to a real person – 'who are you to decide?' – but are now increasingly automated and unaccountable. The mandatory collection of data and biometrics originated with the G8, then permeated down through the US and the EU, with 9/11 allowing a raft of exceptional powers that would never have been dreamed of during the Cold War to become embedded and accepted as the norm.

New governments are only going halfway to reversing this trend. EU governments generally have shifted to the right, while the Obama administration has proved as keen as its predecessor to invoke the notion of state secrecy to block public inquiries and disclosures. Security agents hide behind the cloak of state secrecy, which offers them blanket immunity from prosecution while they delve freely into our lives. The Top Secret America survey estimated that, since

9/11, the official US intelligence budget had tripled to $75 billion, with 263 new bodies of a total of 1,271 government bodies dedicated to countering extremism and with 854,000 people given high-level clearance producing an unreadable 50,000 reports a year.[26]

Good breeding

For centuries, 'good breeding' has underpinned successful horse racing, royalty and racism, and the notion eventually led, supported by the 'sciences' of phrenology and eugenics, to genocides such as the Nazi Holocaust. Now researchers are working on the premise that DNA might not just track down already-existing criminals but also indicate their criminality in advance. According to GeneWatch: 'Numerous research studies have claimed to find genetic links to behavioral traits such as aggression, homosexuality, depression or an addictive personality. None of these studies has stood the test of time.'[27] What matters, however, is who believes in these 'genetic horoscopes'. In 2007, the then-presidential candidate for France Nicolas Sarkozy suggested that pedophiles were 'born that way'. The ensuing uproar led to a swift retraction. However, in the best-selling book *Freakonomics: A Rogue Economist Explores the Hidden Side of Everything*, University of Chicago economist Steven D Levitt contended that US inner city crime rates tumbled in the 1990s mainly because the 1973 Roe vs Wade decision allowed for millions of fetuses, who would have become young criminals, to be aborted instead. This witty notion of the pre-emptive capital punishment of undesirables sold millions and won awards from the likes of the American Economics Association.

A Florida State University study of 2,000 US teens seemed to show that males with a particular form of gene, MAOA, were much more likely to join gangs and use weapons, although the project's director stressed that this did not mean 'everyone with this particular allele is going to be violent and is going to become a gang member – or vice versa'.[28] On every count, greatly complex matrices of historical, environmental and socio-economic forces also have their hand. Even then the data may only reflect, not predict. Answering the question of nature-versus-nurture requires fantastic amounts of data. The Biobank project in the UK seeks to analyse the DNA from 500,000 people and track their lifestyles for a decade, to see how genes and the environment interact to make people ill and what might prevent that. The participants are, however, volunteers, and the protection of their genetic data is sacrosanct.

Computer says go

There is in our culture a growing problem of technological determinism, whereby technology is developed, a justification is found for its use, and everyone then genuflects before its almightiness, allowing the computer to make the decisions. Google is developing an App to trawl employee reviews, promotions and pay histories to predict who might quit. Laszlo Bock, the chief of Google's human resources department, told the *Wall Street Journal* that the algorithm helped the company to 'get inside people's heads even before they know they might leave'.[29] Cataphora has a program to analyze workers' emails, calls and documents for their 'emotive tone'. The program has been developed to meet demand from law firms and management consultants for something to map an office's relationship dynamics, from who is most consulted to who bitches about whom, factoring in workers' attitude according to their use of language or their propensity to write in CAPS.[30] Happy employees are rarely whistle-blowers, whereas disgruntled employees are underperforming, snitching, million-dollar liabilities in waiting – 'Computer says go'.

But could all this money be better spent? In 2009, a survey of incidents filmed by 1,600 CCTV units across Scotland led to immediate police response and arrest just 14 per cent of the time – maybe the £42 million ($65 million) spent on the cameras would have been better spent on 350 extra police officers. The flashy promise of untested technology too often dazzles policy-makers into directing resources that way, without asking whether it will improve on the methods it replaces, let alone taking into account the law of unexpected consequences. As CCTV becomes a 'constant third party in our everyday lives', the ordinary citizen may become less likely to intervene in altercations or take any responsibility for local problems; they may assume that someone else is keeping guard or may not intervene in case their Good Samaritan involvement is recorded and they themselves are charged – CCTV disempowers people.[31] Technology is developed and affects society in curious ways – faster than laws can be passed to regulate it.

Citizens and consumers are exhorted to give up this information and allow its sharing and sale because they should 'trust' the states, banks and companies doing the sharing. Yet the data is also being collected because no-one is to be trusted, and thus people must prove that they are not terrorists or pedophiles in order to do basic good deeds, like voluntary work. The lies that led to the Iraq War and the collapse of the banks have done much to destroy voters' trust in their governments, economies and intelligence services, but the incompetents who presided over these disasters then demand even more data and power in the name of keeping people 'secure'. Meanwhile the masses are amused by being taught to become suspicious of their partners, their children's teachers, their neighbors – to become part of the great game of spying on everyone else. The distrust between citizens, co-workers, commuters, children and teachers grows.

One London school by 2009 had 68 CCTV cameras installed to prevent bullying and theft and to settle any claims made against teachers.[32] In this hyper-monitored world, any youth in a hooded top may be plotting some heinous act, and not just shielding their privacy, and middle-aged men in pubs must remove their Trilby hats so that they can be clearly seen on the CCTV. Distrust becomes normalized, repackaged and marketed as a proper (and profitable) state of mind. The Social Network Integrated Friend Finder (Sniff) was a Facebook application allowing users to track friends and spouses through their mobiles, as if life were just a game.[33]

A government with all its citizens' DNA and every morsel of information about their lives would aspire to develop the ultimate in intrusive, pre-emptive micro-governance. As systems like the European Criminal Records Information System allows member states to share citizens' criminal records and data on suspected terrorists to be become globally accessible, the potential for travelers to be pre-emptively picked up increases. In 2010 Russia allowed its FSB security service to caution citizens for crimes yet to be committed if they were suspected of preparing acts of extremism, or to jail them for obstructing the agency's work – 'a draconian law reminiscent of our repressive past', according to the Solidarity opposition movement.[34]

Surveillance technology can be used to great effect to watch the watchers and keep those in charge in check, as exemplified by the opportune camcorder filming of four Los Angeles police officers beating Rodney King as he lay on the floor – the ensuing trial and acquittal of the officers helped provoke the 1992 LA riots.[35] YouTube broadcasts what the pro-cop *World's Wildest Police Videos* overlooks, like US college library security guards tasering a Middle Eastern student upset at being racially profiled, or another for speaking out at a John Kerry rally in 2007. Cameraphone footage of the Burmese junta's violent crackdown on democracy protestors provoked stern international rebuke for the regime, as did the mobile footage of a protestor being shot dead during Iran's controversial 2009 presidential election.

But there is no escape. The dissenters who spurned the vapidity of the materialistic dystopia depicted in Aldous Huxley's *Brave New World* could at least 'escape' to exile on Iceland. But ECHELON, Facebook, Tesco and Google mean there is really nowhere now to run to – not even to fantasy worlds like Second Life, the online avatar game which allows millions of disillusioned real-world dwellers to virtually 'start again'. Denizens of Second Life do not only start virtual businesses and make virtual marriages, they also employ detectives and bugging devices to trap errant lovers and commit industrial espionage.[36] Private advisors like the Risk Management Group have warned that jihadists could use false IP addresses to use both Second Life and World of Warcraft so as to proselytize, create extremist communities, get funding and train up. Duly concerned, in 2008, the CIA's Project Reynard sought to investigate the malevolent potential and dynamics of such virtual worlds and online games, while Europol and SOCA are also concerned.[37] While Second Life's developer Linden Labs has reported no activity that warrants police interest, and real-life terrorists can use the whole internet to avoid these well-monitored avatar lands, such virtual worlds are appealing real-life labs for those test-driving data-mining projects like Project Reynard. In the search for virtual terrorists, ordinary citizens don't even get a second life online. Nowhere is free from surveillance, in a world where Google is God.

1 Keith Laidler, *Surveillance Unlimited*, Icon, 2008. 2 Ross Anderson, Action on

Rights for Children, http://nin.tl/d8BvXf 3 'Poll shows public disquiet about policing at environmental protests', *The Guardian*, 25 Aug 2009 4 *Evening Standard*, 13 Oct 2009. 5 *The Independent*, 24 Mar 2010, http://nin.tl/amRrcg 6 PBS, http://nin.tl/cl1A1e 7 *Information Week*, 29 Dec 2009, http://nin.tl/cbbGmE 8 www.e-stealth.com & http://nin.tl/bOuRNA 9 John Parker, *Total Surveillance*, Piatkus, 2001. 10 Electronic Privacy Information Center, http://epic.org/privacy/profiling/default.html 11 http://nin.tl/c1v3pf 12 BBC news, 19 Sep 2007, http://nin.tl/9f1rWX 13 eWeek europe, 17 Nov 2009 http://nin.tl/9pcZ8W 14 *The Guardian*, 6 Aug 2006, http://nin.tl/b39EBR 15 John Vanderlippe, CASPIAN www.nocards.org/overview/index.shtml 16 BBC news, 30 Oct 2009, http://nin.tl/98nBeV 17 'Facebook to keep profiles of the dead', AP, 27 Oct 2009. 18 *The First Post*, 27 Nov 2006, http://nin.tl/a62oMN 19 Merle Goldman & Edward X Gu, *Chinese Intellectuals between State and Market*, Routledge, 2004. 20 Greg Walton, International Centre for Human Rights and Democratic Development, Oct 2001. 21 John Reid, 'Liberty, Resilience and Security in a Changing World', 31 Oct 2006. 22 Democracy Now, 28 Jul 2009, http://nin.tl/cTmwcl 23 *Washington Post*, 4 Feb 2010, http://nin.tl/bt8Vc9 24 CNN, 3 May 2010, http://nin.tl/c30GZo 25 'Universities urged to spy on Muslims', *The Guardian*, 16 Oct 2006. 26 *The Guardian*, 19 Jul 2010, http://nin.tl/bRUUFk 27 'Police NDNAD', Genewatch, Jan 2005. 28 '"Gangsta gene" identified in US teens', *New Scientist*, 19 Jun 2009. 29 *Wall Street Journal*, 19 May 2009, http://nin.tl/awlQBr 30 CNN, 24 Sep 2009, http://nin.tl/bjQruY 31 *New Statesman*, 2 Oct 2006, http://nin.tl/9ek8Gs 32 BBC Online, 21 Jul 2009, http://nin.tl/95yNH8 33 *The Times*, 1 Apr 2008, http://nin.tl/dx3xVR 34 *The Guardian*, 29 Jul 2010, http://nin.tl/coivpr 35 See footnote 1. 36 http://nin.tl/cZP6wN 37 http://nin.tl/an9Ukj

Resources

SCORES OF ORGANIZATIONS exist worldwide covering the myriad facets of the very nuanced, subtle and fluid area that is surveillance in all its forms. The websites of the major organizations offering information or the means to protect oneself and others are listed here – but do remember that all your visits to these sites will be logged somewhere!

Based in London and Washington DC, **Privacy International** (www.privacyinternational.org) is a global watchdog organization with two decades of experience in covering surveillance and privacy invasions by governments and corporations. With a similar remit to PI but more Europe-focused in its forensic analyses and news is **Statewatch** (www.statewatch.org), founded in 1991 to cover Europe's legal and not-so-legal stumbling towards super surveillance. **NO2ID** is a UK-based campaign group fighting against ID cards as the vanguard for an altogether more threatening database state. Its website www.no2id.net provides broad analyses, news and lively discussion about the onslaught of surveillance in the UK and beyond.

Amnesty International (www.amnesty.org) is the global NGO for human rights. **The American Civil Liberties Union** is a long-standing, nationwide organization defending Americans' civil rights from the soap-box to the Senate, and its website www.aclu.org is an excellent resource of its campaigns and place amid the history and law of US governmental assaults on freedom and privacy. Its UK-oriented equivalents are **Liberty** (www.liberty-human-rights.org.uk) and the **Joseph Rowntree Foundation** (www.jrf.org.uk). The **Australian Privacy Foundation** (www.privacy.org.au) is an NGO seeking to protect Australians' privacy, and **Civil Liberties Australia** is at www.cla.asn.au. Several organizations focus mainly on the onslaught of surveillance provided by the digital age, from the internet to iPods. US-oriented groups include the **Electronic Frontier Foundation** (www.eff.org) and the **Electronic Privacy Information Center** (www.epic.org). The main organization monitoring surveillance issues in Canada is the Canadian Civil Liberties Association (http://ccla.org), while the New Zealand Council for Civil Liberties can be found at www.nzccl.org.nz. For the UK and EU, there is the **Open Rights Group** (www.openrightsgroup.org).

Regional and linguistic associations seeking political and legal agreements on data protection and privacy include the **Central and Eastern European Data Protection Authority** (www.ceecprivacy.org) founded in 2001 in Warsaw; the **French-Speaking Association of Personal Data Protection Authorities (2007)**, with members from the **Organisation Internationale de la Francophonie** (www.francophonie.org); the **Red Iberoamericana de Proteccion de Datos** (www.redipd.org) set up in 2003 with the concept of personal data protection espoused as a Fundamental Right. The EU's energies on data protection are channeled through the **European Data Protection Supervisor** (www.edps.europa.eu/EDPSWEB).

Most of the resources above have information and guidance as to how individuals may legally or technologically shield themselves from intrusive surveillance. For example, the EFF's online **Surveillance Self-Defense** project is at https://ssd.eff.org Meanwhile, **www.allfacebook.com** is a tidy blog-watch of Facebook and offers tips to avoid allowing it to reveal all. **Google Watch** (www.google-watch.org) is a somewhat scatty collation of anti-Google articles and opinion pieces.

While **GeneWatch**'s main interest is GM food and farming (www.genewatch.org), it is also extensively involved in the debate about the growth and use of DNA databases, while **www.leavethemkidsalone.com** and **www.leavethemkidsalone.com/usa.htm** give good links to stories about the growth of surveillance and biometrics aimed at children. **Action on Rights for Children** (www.archrights.org.uk) is a more measured look at the legal rights.

The **World Summit on the Information Society** was a UN project held in 2003 and 2005 aimed at bridging the digital divide between the rich and poor nations by working to bring half the world's poor online by 2015 (www.itu.int/wsis/index.html). How the world's governments and partners will bring that about is detailed by the **Internet Governance Forum** (www.intgovforum.org). News and PR from the industry of surveillance (although its purveyors prefer to refer to their world as security), identity and risk management can be found through **www.findbiometrics.com** and **www.securityinfowatch.com**

Index

Index

Index

Index